TALES OF A WELL-SPENT YOUTH

PART 2

THE COLLEGE YEARS

TALES OF A WELL-SPENT YOUTH

PART 2

THE COLLEGE YEARS

Cal McGoogan

ABOOKS

Alive Book Publishing

Tales of a Well-Spent Youth, Volume 2
The College Years
Copyright © 2021 by Cal McGoogan

Additional copies may be ordered from the publisher for educational, business, promotional or premium use. For information, contact ALIVE Book Publishing at: alivebookpublishing.com, or call (925) 837-7303.

Cover Art by Angelica McGoogan
Book Design by Alex Johnson

ISBN 13
978-1-63132-121-4 Paperback
978-1-63132-123-8 EBook

Library of Congress Control Number: 2020915524

Library of Congress Cataloging-in-Publication Data
is available upon request.

First Edition

Published in the United States of America by ALIVE Book Publishing and ALIVE Publishing Group, imprints of Advanced Publishing LLC 3200 A Danville Blvd., Suite 204, Alamo, California 94507 alivebookpublishing.com

PRINTED IN THE UNITED STATES OF AMERICA

10 9 8 7 6 5 4 3 2 1

Chapter 1
Off to College

With the beginning of freedom comes the baggage from internment

Kelly was off to college (freedom) in his bronze '73 Pinto (the Pimpo mobile). He left Grandma's house in Coral Gables with his coin collection, his stamp collection, and his Beatles albums. Kelly was still at odds with his dad, Kelly Sr. Their only contact was at Kelly Jr.'s apartment during the summer when Kelly Sr. decided to show up, show his presence, and show that he knew where Kelly lived. It was all about "show." Kelly Sr. walked away and got in his truck once Kelly Jr. stepped out onto the second floor balcony to greet him. "I know where you live," Kelly Sr. announced.

That was all behind Kelly Jr. now that he was headed off to college and a new life. Kelly also had a few 45 records that he used to carry around with a belt through the large hole of the small 45s. He remembered that the first 45 record purchased in his youth was the Archie's "Sugar, Sugar." It was lost somewhere along the line.

Anyway, the 200-mile drive to the Cloud City was uneventful, but as it was September, it was smoking hot in a piece of crap car with no A/C and broken plastic seats. You are probably saying, "Why Cloud City? That's not where college is." Kelly knew there was little parking on campus, so Kelly asked Rob (his best friend from high school) if he could leave the Pimpo in Cloud City for the upcoming fall quarter. So the Pimpo stayed in Rob's parents' garage for three months.

Rob wasn't starting the Naval Academy until late September.

So Kelly asked Rob, "Can you drop me off in Tallytown?" Rob said, "Of course. That will give us a day or two to hang out before your school starts." They took off for Tallytown in Rob's sky blue Bug, otherwise known as a Beetle. The Beetle had no A/C either, so the trip up the turnpike and over onto US 27 was unbearable. On US 27 Rob and Kelly passed the reptile zoo and crossed over the Fenholloway River. The Fenholloway was where Kelly's grandparents had their first date on a paddle wheel ship.

But where is Smith Hall? Wow! Old and smelly, but a towering yellow brick on the hill. It was once the tallest building between Jacksonville and Pensacola. Smith Hall was demolished thirty years after Kelly stayed there for a quarter.

Kelly and Rob hit the hotspots of Tallytown at the time: Fred's Backdoor Lounge (it had no usable backdoor) and Jack's Roadhouse (there were no motorcycles). Then Rob took off back to the Cloud City, leaving Kelly to fend for himself. Fun, fun, fun!

Kelly's dorm roommate showed up two days before classes started. Dave was older than most college students. He was mature and quiet. Dave didn't talk much but had a late '60s Mustang to get around town. Perfect!

That afternoon a knock came at the dormitory door. Who can that be? It was Greg and Patrick. "Hey we're from the fraternity Pi Phi. We're having a party tonight. Why don't you stop by?" Was this to be the beginning of new experience in Kelly's life? He obviously didn't think so at the time. Could it end up being a good experience and also a bad experience? The answer was yes. Events are Coming Soon to a book near you.

Greg was a heavyset blonde guy who was very personable and convincing. Patrick was his sidekick, tall and dark-haired with lots of energy. They were roommates in the fraternity house, each with his own waterbed. Waterbeds were the bomb at the time.

Greg wasn't going to leave Kelly's dorm room door until

Kelly agreed to show up at the frat party. Greg was persuasive and friendly with an underlying air of insistence. Kelly couldn't say no. "OK, where is it? If you can pick me up, I'll be there. I have no car." It turned out that the house was way on the other side of campus. The pickup and ride came in handy.

The party consisted of all the fraternity brothers and "little sisters." Kelly asked Greg, "Why are they called *little* sisters?" Greg responded that sororities had sisters and the *little* sister differentiated the two. Kelly thought, "That sounds a bit sexist." It became clear to Kelly later that little sisters of PiPhi were associated with the fraternity but not actual members. They came to the house for parties and gatherings and were encouraged to feel part of something bigger.

There were sixteen brothers living in the old, two-story, wood frame house. In addition there were six or seven brothers living off campus. These off-site brothers still came around for the parties, but had tired of living in the frat house proper.

The party had a keg of beer in the kitchen along with red punch in a trash bag inside a kitchen trash pail. Kelly decided to try the punch. It had floating fruit and tasted like cherry Kool Aid. Kelly told Greg, "I can't really taste the alcohol in the punch." Greg responded, "That's the plan, man." Kelly later found out that a couple gallons of vodka went into each punch concoction and the girls loved it.

Kelly made contacts with a couple girls during the party, but girls were not on his "to-do list" at the time. Besides, he was technically still dating his girlfriend Dana who had another year of high school back in Orlando. His main focus was studying hard and making good grades so he could get into med school. Kelly's maternal grandfather had been a physician and Kelly's mother Liza wanted him to follow in his grandfather's tracks. Kelly had worked with his dad, Kelly Sr., in his optometry office and didn't like it. "Better here? Better there?" All day long. But optometry remained a second option as post-graduate schooling.

Kelly soon fell into a routine. There were classes in the day. On weeknights he used the university library for homework and studying between 7 and 10pm. On weekends, Friday and Saturday night gatherings at the fraternity were in order.

Chapter 2
The Fraternity

*When you encounter a schoolyard bully,
you can eat your lunch in the library for the rest of your life,
or you can stand up and fight back.*

There were fraternity houses and then there were fraternity HOUSES. There were literally tall white mansions and "little shacks." The PiPhi house was more like a shack, but the upper crust frat brothers lived in pillared two-story manors. Their houses looked like something out of *Gone with the Wind*.

Fraternities like the Pikes occupied these halls of opulence. The movie *Animal House* had not come out yet, but it was as if the producers had come to the PiPhi house and then written the script. The scene of the brothers sitting around the house's living room and John Belushi trying to rally the troops was right out of a PiPhi . event.

Many of the fraternity brothers were business majors. Somehow the Business School managed to pack all of its classes into Monday through Thursday. This meant that business majors had all day Friday off from school. For the brothers this was an early start to weekend partying. Their curriculum didn't seem all that demanding either, especially for a pre-med student like Kelly.

But Kelly would nevertheless show up at the fraternity on Friday afternoons to drink beer and throw the Frisbee on car-active College Avenue. Brother Kyle was a senior headed back to Louisiana for medical school. His father was a doctor back home, and Kelly was sure that a few strings had been pulled to get Kyle into med school. Regardless, Kyle provided the beer every Friday afternoon on the front porch of the fraternity. The beers were kept by the hanging deck chair where Kyle sat.

The street Frisbee tossing began after a few beers. The routine call was "Car!!" to keep the brothers from getting run over in the street. Harrison was Kelly's main Frisbee partner and later billiards competitor. The afternoon beer drinking turned into Friday evening drinking. The house had a rule that marijuana could not be consumed inside the frat house. That didn't keep a few of the brothers, including Harrison, from sneaking a joint in the backyard. Kelly had tried pot before and it always made him feel paranoid. "Why did he say that? Why is she looking at me that way?" That didn't seem like fun to Kelly.

The brothers would have chapter meetings on Sunday nights. Kelly was not privy to those meetings, but there was a decision to invite ten individuals into the brotherhood. Eight students agreed to pledge the fraternity, one of which was Kelly. Being a Pi Phi pledge seemed like a dream to Kelly, as much positive attention was paid to him and the other pledges. However, negative attention was in the works.

One afternoon all the pledges were lined up by the brothers into the house living room. Yelling began as if the pledges were in drill training. Cigars were lit by the brothers and blown into the faces of each pledge. Kelly decided he wasn't going to take this nonsense and walked out. He made it up the sidewalk to the Westcott fountain with Greg following him. Greg caught up and used his charm and patience to calm Kelly down. Kelly didn't go back to the house that day, but agreed to come back on a different day. Maybe he should have kept on walking.

Kelly drew away from the fraternity life for a little while. His roommate Dave and he would take Dave's Mustang out for dinner on Friday nights. But eventually Kelly went back to the frat house at the coaxing of Greg.

Parties sometimes got out of hand. One night Kelly had too much to drink and was lain down on the plastic couch in the entryway. This meant that everyone coming or going saw him lying in a drunken stupor, passed out on the couch. One of the brothers had placed a plastic trash pail next to Kelly in case there was an accident. Kelly had no intention of throwing up until he smelled the cigarette butt fumes wafting from the trash can. There it goes, puke city. Maybe that was a good thing for the following day's health.

During one of the later weekend parties, brother Perry was trying to chat up one of the potential little sisters on the couch in the living room. It was clear that Kate had more interest in Kelly than in Perry. In fact, during the next quarter, Kelly became Kate's *big* brother. Kelly turned out to be a poor big brother to Kate, but that is in the future.

Perry became emotionally jealous of Kelly in the kitchen of the house and the two began a short-lived fistfight. Kelly's watch broke in the process and hateful words were spewed. From that point on the two maintained a ready-to-burst dislike for each other. Luckily, Perry's roommate Charles fixed Kelly's watch. Another love triangle where "he liked her, and she liked the other him," but Kelly was indifferent.

Chapter 3
The Countdown to Hell Week

Brotherhood can be a gift from heaven or a scourge from hell.

L ife continued on, pretty much as drawn up, books and beer with the hope of making good grades and becoming a PiPhi brother. Pledges were expected to wear a PiPhi pin on their shirts when on campus. The pin said "PiPhi pledge." It was a small form of defamation to the individual, and Kelly refused to wear it. One day at the student union Kelly was observed to not be wearing his pledge pin by Brother Charles. Charles asked, "Why aren't you wearing your pledge pin?" And this was even before *Animal House!* Kelly replied, "Because I don't want to wear it." Kelly had always been a bit of a rebel. Kelly didn't get spit on with the "Pppledge Pppin" antic, but Charles wasn't happy. He didn't push it and left Kelly to do what he wanted.

Seminole football was a great escape on Saturday nights. The team was having a winning season under a new head coach (BB) after many years of losing seasons. All the fraternities including PiPhi walked to Doak Campbell stadium and sat with their brotherhood. Usually a pint of rum was smuggled into the stadium in the sport socks of the individual named Kelly. The PiPhis all sat together and yelled their fraternal chants and proclamations. One chant of note started, "We are the PiPhi raiders, raiders of the night, we're dirty sons of bitches, we'd rather f*** than fight!" Kelly stopped bringing bottles into the stadium when he observed a drunken person throw a glass bottle down the stands. The bottle hit a girl in the back of the head and she had to be carted away. No more bottles for Kelly, not that he would ever replicate this kind of event.

The pledges were lined up occasionally in the frat house and made to answer trivial questions about the fraternity and the chapter. This didn't bother Kelly, because there were no cigars and no yelling. But one event was looming and everyone knew it: Hell Week.

Kelly's pledge class brothers were a very diverse group, but all were white. The PiPhi fraternity had deviated from the unstated segregation of white and black fraternities in the past. Kelly saw pictures in the house of past black brothers. PiPhi was a small chapter at FSU and they wanted all types of brothers. That was unheard of in those days, but PiPhi had bucked the system and Kelly liked that. It reminded him of his own unconventional ways. Plus no one had to get a branded omega symbol on their arm.

Some of the standout pledges in Kelly's pledge class were Herbert, Ike, Tony, and Noah. Herbert spoke what was on his mind but with a laugh and a smile to go with it. The assumption was that Herbert was gay, but rarely did someone come out of the closet in those days. Herbert became one of Kelly's apartment roommates in the spring of his freshman year. In later years their suspicions were assumed to be factual when Herbert moved to Key West. Key West was the up-and-coming Castro District of San Francisco. Ike stated what was on his mind with small snippets, even though nothing he said seemed to pertain to what was currently happening. His head would slant the other way with each proclamation.

Tony was soft-spoken with great semi-wavy light brown hair. Tony was into LP albums and kept them in a wooden crate built especially for their storage. Kelly told Tony, "That box is a really good idea." Kelly was also into LPs and soon built a similar storage box for his long playing records. But Kelly took it two steps further by varnishing his box and applying a lockable latch to the lid and box. Noah was from Miami with family roots in NYC. He hated the Dallas Cowboys because they had once beaten his beloved Miami Dolphins in the Super Bowl. He was the shortest of the pledges and always stood at the end of the pledge lineup. Alpha Epsilon Pi had a house three doors away from PiPhi, so Kelly once asked Noah, "Why didn't you pledge AEPi?" Noah's response was, "They didn't want me and rejected me as a possible brother." It was true! PiPhi was a bunch of discards, except Kelly, of course.

A block away from the fraternity house was an old cemetery with large stand-up headstones. One night the pledges were ordered to go the graveyard and find items for the brotherhood. The cemetery was pitch black and empty of live humans. Kelly figured out what was going on when brothers began appearing from behind gravestones. The brother would bark out a line of fraternal wisdom with a flashlight pointing at his chin. The pledges had to collect all the items and bring them back to the frat house. It took a couple hours to find all the brothers with objects. Kinda scary but what a waste of time!

Hell Week was announced to be the first week of December prior to final exams. Pledges would continue to go to their classes, but had to spend nights at the fraternity. One day Dana, Kelly's girlfriend from home, called him on the frat house phone. How did she get the number? Anyway, Kelly knew it was over and saw her over Thanksgiving break after hitching a ride home. Kelly took her out for a meal and then told her the bad news. Dana held back tears, and said she had to go inside her house for a minute. She returned with Kelly's high school ring that she had worn on her finger with an inserted tightening device. The two never saw each other until later in life, but it was clear Dana took it very hard. Thirty years later after getting together with Dana, Dana announced to the waiter, the bartender and anyone she saw, "This guy broke up with me!" And there was no alcohol involved! She was obviously still hurt after all that time. Time does not heal all wounds.

During the Thanksgiving holiday, Kelly retrieved his car from Rob's house and thanked Rob's mom and dad for keeping the Pimpo. Kelly hung out over the Thanksgiving weekend with his high school buds. There was an outdoor party in the woods with many ex-high schoolers. Rob was there with his usual bottle of Southern Comfort. Rob got pretty wasted, so Kelly and Rog had to take him home. Once there, Rob's dad asked them, "How come you guys can maintain but Rob is always hammered?" Rob's dad was cool and knew what we were up to. Kelly didn't think Rob got much alcohol practice as a freshman at the Naval Academy and that probably created the resistance difference. After the Thanksgiving holiday, Kelly drove the Pimpo back to Tallytown for a very busy two weeks.

The first Sunday night in December started Hell Week. The pledges were put together in a corner of the frat house game room on the carpeted floor, bordered by two walls and two couches placed together at right angles. They had individually brought pillows and blankets to sleep in this area. The pledges were asked if they wanted to shower. The answer had to be unanimous because the premise was that the pledges were a team. Kelly wanted to shower, and replied "Yes," but the other pledges replied "No." This upset the brotherhood and Kelly fell in line with the "No" answer to make one voice. The 'No' answer was because the house was very cold with a failing heater for the entire house. The tap water was also known to go cold.

With that settled, the pledges were left in the space assigned to them with the assumption that they would get a night's sleep before heading off to classes in the morning. But what were those five-foot speakers doing just outside the couches? The pledges found out soon enough. Just after all pledges had fallen asleep around midnight, the speakers blared out at a full 10 volume, "Up against the wall mother f***er!" The pledges were lined up in their sleepy state for a verbal brandishing by some

of the brothers. The brothers who enjoyed this the most were recent inductees to the frat who wanted to get some revenge for
what they had had to go through during their pledge period.

Back to the sleeping space for the pledges to be allowed sleep
the rest of the night. Of course, not much sleep was gained due
to the expectation of blaring music at any minute. It didn't come
that night, but each of the following nights contained a large,
wee hour cacophony from the huge speakers next to the couches.
This arrangement ensured that none of the pledges slept on the
couches. Besides, that wouldn't be 'team' play.

Classes over the next three days were hard to endure, but the
pledges were happy to get out of the fraternity house and escape
Hell Week for a brief time. Kelly thought about leaving the situation many times. He wasn't sure he could take the treatment
for a whole week, but figured he had made it this far so he
would stick it out.

Surprisingly, on Wednesday evening the routine of the last
three days changed. The pledges were whisked into the living
room and lined up as usual. This was definitely different, as
semi-drunken brothers asked individual pledges to drink with
them. Beers and liquor were provided, usually from the same
containers that the brothers were drinking from. Each brother
who was present asked each pledge "Will you drink with me?"
The pledges were reticent at first, but one drink led to another
and everyone was pretty much hammered within a half hour. It
sure beat sitting in that walled off space for another night waiting for the music to blast.

At the end of these shenanigans, the president brother, also
known as the archon, waltzed in with an announcement. "Hell
Week is over! Initiation into the brotherhood will begin!" Kelly
didn't remember much about what happened next due to the alcohol and lack of sleep other than it was a well-planned extrav-
aganza. In addition, he was extolled not to reveal the initiation
ceremony events with his hand on a Bible. The other thing that

was to remain undisclosed among PiPhi brothers was the secret handshake and the mantra stated during the handshake.

At the end of these initiation rituals, all pledges were gathered together. It was announced that they were all PiPhi brothers now and forever. The celebration of hugging and more drinks ensued. It was a great feeling of being part of something bigger.

Chapter 4
Moving into the Fraternity House

Time wounds all heals. The wounds always fester.

Kelly aced his final exams for the fall quarter, receiving all As for his classes. These were mostly liberal arts classes since he was an underclassman and studies would eventually get much harder in upcoming years. With that said, the euphoria of achieving good grades while pledging a fraternity was very satisfying.

Kelly decided to move into the fraternity house for the winter semester. His bunk bed roommate would be Edward and they would share an upstairs room next to the bathroom. The room had a bunk bed, a desk, two built-in closets, and built-in drawers for clothing. Kelly was assigned the upper bunk. This should be a great situation for rooming, as Edward was hardly ever around. He was off pursuing his military career through ROTC training and other soldierly activities. Edward always rose at the break of dawn to attend his ROTC and class activities. Kelly tried to sleep through the dressing activities by Edward, but he was only semi-successful. Even the pillow covering Kelly's head was of little comfort.

Kelly had been worried about finances during his first quarter and had tried the ROTC route. The promise was that the US Army would finance his college tuition and Kelly would then pay back the loan with two years of military service. There was no Navy or Air Force ROTC on campus, so Army was the only choice. It seemed like a good idea at the time. Vietnam was over and there were no threats of imminent wars.

Mondays and Wednesdays required a one-hour class of military history, procedures, and coercive discussions. But every Friday Kelly would have to dress in a military uniform for outdoor activities. Each ROTC student would line up in rows on the open field. The uniformed student on the end of each row would respond to the shouting sergeant, "Five cadets accounted for!" If you made a mistake and called the sergeant "Sir," he would get in your face and derisively yell that he was to be addressed as sergeant, not sir!

Kelly was new to the line-up process as it was his first quarter in trying ROTC. One Friday he made the mistake of positioning himself at the end of a row. The sergeant yelled at him, "All present and accounted for?" Kelly was speechless and froze. The shouted order came again, "All present and accounted for?" Kelly did not respond, just then realizing he had mistakenly stood at the row's end. By this time the sergeant was in Kelly's face berating him to answer. Kelly's independent character kicked in by then, and he purposely refused to answer. The sergeant gave up on Kelly and moved to the next row with his tirade. At that point Kelly thought his ROTC training could be short-lived.

Kelly's thinking was cemented later in his ROTC training when he had to run a track mile in military boots and he had to rappel down a fifty-foot wooden structure using a hand-held rope. It was bad enough climbing up fifty feet, much less climbing down the structure with no safety ropes and some upper classmen yelling at him, "Get off my tower, you scumbucket!!"

Kelly did not sign up for Army ROTC the following quarter. He decided he would have to pay his college tuition some other way. But he did give credit to those like his new roommate Edward who could handle the physical and mental challenges placed before them. ROTC just wasn't for him.

Before the fraternity house move-in happened in January, Kelly said goodbye to Dave, his Smith Hall roommate, and packed up the Pimpo for the drive back to Cloud City. Kelly was still not talking to his dad, so he spent the Christmas holiday with his friend Tuck. Tuck had a two-bedroom rental in a duplex home. Tuck had been the Methodist Youth Fellowship director when Kelly attended MYF events on Sunday afternoons. Tuck and Kelly had maintained a friendship over the months and years.

The days usually started at Eckerd's Drug Store for breakfast. Then back at Tuck's house, Rob and Rog would show up to indulge in the five-pound bag of pistachios that Kelly's mom Liza had given him for Christmas. Liza had been providing Kelly with $100 a month for his first three months of college. Liza then suddenly stopped supporting Kelly when she left her third husband, Ricky. It was time to look for husband #4. Luckily Grandma was sending Kelly $200 a month. Grandma supported Kelly through four years of undergraduate university, and he would be eternally grateful.

One night at Tuck's, Rob got really smashed. Rog was supposed to come over but apparently he got distracted or waylaid at his parents' house. Rob became livid, yelling obscenities about Rog. Rob proceeded to punch a hole in Tuck's wall. The next day was spent hung over, spackling a hole in Tuck's drywall.

Tuck became very interested in Kelly's stories about Seminole land and the fraternity. Kelly didn't know it, but Tuck had made up his mind to go back to school, finish his degree, and join a fraternity. It turned out Tuck later pledged to the PiPhis. Welcome Tuck!

A new quarter started with Kelly living in the PiPhi fraternity house. There was parking at the house, so Kelly now had transportation using the Pimpo. Back in those days, there were no ATMs, so people would wait in long car lines at the bank to make their vacuumed transactions. While waiting in one of those now outdated lines the Ford Pinto spontaneously caught fire. All the surrounding cars dispersed quickly because of the bad reputation Pintos had. However in this case Kelly's Pinto wasn't hit from behind and didn't blow up. The bank security guards came out with extinguishers and put out the engine fire. Kelly was carless again.

Chapter 5
Illness and Reconciliation

There are two sides to everyone's heart, good and bad.
The one that wins is fed the most.

The upstairs brothers liked to congregate and BS in the foyer outside of their four bedrooms. There were a couple chairs and a couch. It was cold in the house because Greg couldn't get the furnace going. For some reason the brothers didn't use space heaters. They just endured the January freezing.

During one of the social gatherings among the upstairs brothers, Herbert was eating Ritz Crackers. Herbert offered the crackers to the other relaxers. Kelly accepted a few crackers from the box that Herbert was eating out of and breathing on. A few days later it was announced to the brotherhood that Herbert was in the Leon County Hospital with meningitis. His hospital phone number was posted for all to wish him well. Kelly made the call to Herbert and was glad that he was doing OK.

A few days later Kelly began feeling sick. Kelly was vomiting and could not keep anything down, not even water. But, he made it on his own to the campus medical office. The visit was free, included in his tuition, so that was a blessing. The doctor at the small clinic had no idea what was wrong with Kelly, but he provided a penicillin injection for possible infection. Kelly's infection was later determined to be bacterial, so according to future doctors, the penicillin likely saved his life.

Kelly continued to vomit, so Greg and Patrick as co-big brothers for Kelly took him to the hospital emergency room. Kelly was throwing up in the back seat of Greg's car the whole way there. It was a watery retch that went onto the floor of the car.

Once arriving at the ER, a physician with a large cowboy hat examined Kelly and found nothing wrong. A simple request for Kelly to touch his chest with his chin would have let the cowboy doctor know what was up. Dr. "Big hat with no cattle" sent Kelly home with no treatment.

The next morning Kelly was worse than ever and his big brothers took him back to the ER. This time a competent doctor tested Kelly with the chin to chest request. Kelly could not make the move and the knowledgeable doctor knew immediately what was wrong. Kelly was instantly admitted to the ICU for meningitis.

Herbert was now better from his meningitis bout and left the hospital. Kelly began to receive his treatment that stopped the vomiting and let him sleep a lot. Kelly also received calls from the brotherhood wishing him well. The one call that stood out was from Kevin sending a heartfelt "Get Well." Kelly and Kevin didn't always get along, but brotherhood overrode any negativity between the two.

During Kelly's first few weeks of living in the fraternity house there was a man who would pass by on the sidewalk and enter the apartment building next door. He sometimes would stop and chat with any PiPhi brothers on the front porch or sidewalk. He introduced himself to Kelly as Chris. Kelly thought nothing of it as the guy was clean-shaven, well-dressed but older than most college students. Chris seemed interested in college girls and would ask about the best way to meet them. The east side of campus was filled with sorority houses and apparently this was the path that Chris took.

While Kelly was in the ICU at Tallahassee Leon, he heard of the murders and bludgeoning of sorority sisters at the Chi Omega sorority. Two sorority sisters were murdered, Margaret Bowman and Lisa Levy. The initial two attacks were on the survivors, Karen Chandler and Kathy Kleiner. These two miraculous survivors were down the hall from Kelly while he was in the ICU battling meningitis. Luckily Karen, Kathy, and Kelly all survived their inflictions, though inflicted in two very different ways.

One day in the hospital, Kelly was a bit out of it, but in walked his dad, Kelly Sr., and his stepmother, "Mom." They had driven up to Tallahassee to visit Kelly in the hospital. Kelly burst into tears and said, "What we went through was stupid, stupid, stupid." Hugs ensued and the relationship between Kelly and his parents was repaired. This was an emotional example of how bad things can turn into good things.

Kelly was feeling much better one day in the hospital and began to touch himself. He had no idea that he was always on camera while in the ICU. The ER doctor and his personal nurse walked in and the doctor said, "It looks like you may be ready to go home." Kelly didn't understand this reference until he was walking out of the hospital saw all the TV screens at the nurse's station. How embarrassing!

Kelly went back to the freezing fraternity house committed to leaving the house at the end of the quarter.

Chapter 6

Back to the Books and an Awful Realization

I can't stand to see a grown man hit a woman.
No matter what the woman did, or in this case, what she didn't do.

Kelly went back to the fraternity house and tried to salvage what he could of his classes after being gone for two weeks. Unbelievably, Tuck, who was now pledging the fraternity, had gone and spoken with all of Kelly's professors, explaining his situation. Due to this heartfelt action by Tuck, all of the professors were open to Kelly making up what he had missed.

Kelly worked hard at his studies to keep from losing an entire quarter, and he was successful. At the end of the quarter Kelly received a report card in the mail posting all As and Bs for the winter quarter. But let's not get ahead of ourselves.

The winter quarter continued with indoor weekend parties at the fraternity house. Kelly was especially attracted to a girl named Gloria with short, cropped reddish brown hair. Her personality was very attractive as were her physical attributes and smile. The only problem with that Gloria was that she was the girlfriend of one of the winter pledges. Hmmm…

No one had seen the neighbor Chris in a while but then again nobody thought much of it. People came and went all the time at a major university. Some people flunk out, some can't stand the loneliness of being away from home, some don't have the tuition, but not many leave because they have cudgeled and murdered four sorority sisters.

In February of that winter quarter '78 Ted Bundy was caught in Pensacola, leaving Florida for Alabama. His picture was painted across the media, including newspapers and television. Kelly and the PiPhi brothers were stunned, shocked and at a loss for words. This picture showed Chris, their neighbor from West College Avenue. A mass murderer had been in their midst and no one knew it. It was chilling to say the least. As the investigations moved on and it was certain that Ted Bundy had been the sordid perpetrator of the Chi Omega attacks and murders, Kelly bought and wore a t-shirt showing an electric chair with the statement "Burn Bundy Burn." People were solemn, but supportive of the shirt.

Gloria continued to attend all the weekend activities at the house since her boyfriend was pledging the fraternity and had to be there. Gloria would be on her own at the house most of the time while her boyfriend was busy with fraternal issues. They had been dating a long while (back to high school) and he seemed to take Gloria for granted, while she seemed to be open to a new relationship. Kelly and Gloria were drawn to each other every time they talked. Conditions seemed right for a change. This flirtation continued through the winter weeks, but Gloria would need to make a decision. She thought to herself, "Should I make a change and see Kelly or should I stick with a boring situation?" The spring quarter would tell.

As mentioned before, Kelly did really well in school that winter quarter, but spring break was imminent. Two weeks of freedom and fun were on the way!

Chapter 7
A Visit to Mexico

Fun! Fun! Fun! 'Til the Federales take your Mazda away.

Rob's spring break lined up perfectly with Kelly's and they planned a trip to San Diego to visit Kelly's brother Skip. Skip had made a friend in the Army named Billy who was from the San Diego area. They started a business coifing hair, but Skip and Billy wanted to take some time off and visit Baja, Mexico. Rob and Kelly flew out to San Diego from Orlando to meet up. The only vehicle Skip and Billy had was a two-seater MG. So Kelly rented a brand new, black, two-seater Mazda RX7. It even had a sliding sunroof. Billy and Skip were smart to take the older POS vehicle into Mexico, but let the amusement begin!

Billy's family had a house trailer permanently kept in a Puerto Nuevo trailer park. This would be the group's home base for the next few days. Puerto Nuevo was just south of Rosarito but north of Ensenada, Baja Mexico. To get there the two coupe cars left San Diego south on I-5. They stayed driving together and crossed the border with a wave from a Mexican border guard. No long lines to get into Mexico. Ha-ha! That put them into the traffic of Tijuana where nobody paid any attention to any traffic lights. Each signaled intersection was backed up in all directions. The next intersection crossing was made by the driver with the biggest cajones. You could be waiting a long time if you were behind someone with small ones.

This was in the days before cell phones but the two small cars managed to stay together using nerves of steel or with the other metal: brass balls. Kelly had a map to the trailer, as he didn't want to take any chances in a foreign country. The road led out to the Pacific along the Tijuana River. Then there seemed to be a road choice going south between a pay-for-use road and a free road. As usual the Pay Road was non-stop and empty while the free road was packed with cars and many stops along the way. No one had any pesos so they had to stay on the free road which added an extra hour and mucho descaro.

The four anticipators of merriment arrived at their destination and took down their bags. Skip and Billy had the two small bedrooms, while Kelly and Rob were assigned the two couches. Kelly said, "It doesn't matter, we can sleep anywhere after partaking in Mexican elixir. The first question out of everyone's mouth was, "Where is the tequila?" Billy had brought a bottle of cheap Jose Cuervo, but Jose Cuervo was no friend of Kelly's. Kelly asked, "Where's the local bar?"

Luckily there was a local hangout within walking distance. The front door was open to the street and the open backdoor looked out onto the sand of the Pacific Ocean. What a sight! The Tecate and the Pacifico bottles began draining. It was a little early for tequila shots, especially when the local horse handler asked the bar patrons if anyone wanted to take a ride on the beach. All four travelers said yes. If you've never ridden a horse on the sand of a beach, venturing near the ocean water, put it on your bucket list!

The group went back to the trailer house with a few take-out beers. The rest of the day was spent lounging in the patio sun. A couple cheap tequila shots and everyone was ready for bed. Rob and Kelly had seen scores of bumper stickers in San Diego advertising Hussong's Cantina and a bar called Papa's and Beer. Apparently the two cantinas were within walking distance of each other in Ensenada. This was Rob and Kelly's agenda for the next day.

Everyone was slow to get up the next morning. Rob stumbled down the front door steps and called out, "Who ate the corn, man?" Apparently someone, who would go nameless, threw up on the steps. Rob and Kelly climbed out of their hangovers around noon and decided that they were headed to Ensenada. Skip and Billy were veterans of the touristy town and said, "Vaya con dios."

Rob and Kelly climbed into the brand new RX7 and headed south on the toll version of 1D. When they pulled into the town of Ensenada the place was hopping. It was a Saturday and it looked like half of San Diego had shown up. The streets were crowded around their destination of Hussong's. There appeared to be no street parking until Kelly spotted an empty space across the street. He used the maneuvering of the little car to make a U-turn and park in the spot.

The U-turn was a big no-no in downtown Ensenada and a street policeman immediately showed up with a ticket notebook and pen in hand. The policeman did not issue a ticket, as he knew the gringos would never pay it. He said, "Driver's license, por favor." When Kelly handed over his license to the policeman he said, "You can retrieve your license at the police station, two blocks that away." He pointed and walked away with the license.

Kelly said, "Crap, I'll just get a new license when I get home. Wait, how am I going to get on the airplane home with no ID? Guess we'll have to stop by the police station and pay the fine before leaving town. Let's go to Hussong's!"

Hussong's was a dump. There was an ancient, scraped-up bar along one entire wall. Some scroungy chairs littered the room. The single floor room had a high ceiling. The boys sidled up to the bar and ordered beers, whatever was cheap. The bartender had attitude toward Kelly and Rob. He was likely sick of Americanos telling him what to do. He reluctantly drew two Carta Blancas from a dirty tap and plopped them down on the bar. The bartender said, "One hundred pesos." The boys had only American money and dropped five dollars on the bar, which was readily accepted.

Hussong's contained mostly older folks, huddled with each other and just looking around. It was obvious they were there as tourists who just wanted to see the famous attraction. Kelly was sure it was a big let- down for them. There was no partying going on, so Kelly and Rob had another beer and said, "Let's get out of here."

Right down the street with the Pacific Ocean in view was Papas and Beer. The establishment had two bars, one downstairs and on upstairs. The upstairs was crowded with music and some folks dancing. Kelly said, "Now we're talking!" The beers and tequila shots were flowing. It appeared that most of the crowd was from a cruise boat because at around 4pm most everyone got up and left. But, before that occurrence Kelly had his eye on a cute girl who was sitting with her family around a crowded table. Kelly decided he would ask her to dance. The pretty girl came out from behind the table in a wheel chair. After the initial shock, she and Kelly proceeded to the dance area. She wheeled around in her chair in time with the music and Kelly danced in front of her. When the song ended, Kelly escorted her back to her family's table. The family was so happy. They hugged Kelly and thanked him for his understanding. Kelly would never forget that as one of those events that truly affect your life.

Rob congratulated Kelly for his understanding. After a couple more beers it was time to head back to Puerto Nuevo. The boys walked back up the street toward the RX7. Kelly noticed that the same street officer was walking around. Kelly asked him, "Do you still have my license?' The policeman replied in the affirmative. Kelly flashed a five dollar bill. The cop got very nervous and looked around. He then waved Kelly to a nearby alley where the transaction occurred, five bucks for a Florida driver's license.

Kelly and Rob got into the Mazda and headed out of town. They were mildly buzzed after an afternoon of beer drinking, but OK to drive. About halfway back to the house trailer, a motorcycle cop was apparently attracted to the brand new car with California plates. He blazed his blue lights and siren, pulling the boys over. La huda didn't ask for registration or license. He only said, "Vente, vente. You drunk. You drunk". Kelly had been a student of Spanish in high school and college, so he knew this was a demand for twenty dollars American. The boys were low on cash after an afternoon of beer drinking. Rob opened his wallet and saw two one-dollar bills. He rolled up the bills and handed them to the cop. The cop took the bills after Rob showed him an empty wallet. The motorcycle cop got back on it and rode away. Little did the cop know that Rob and Kelly kept their real money in the hidden pockets of their wallets.

Kelly and Rob were in unbelievable amazement, but were happy and drove on. A couple miles from their destination of Puerto Nuevo, the same motorcycle cop was on the side of the road with his lights flashing. He motioned for Kelly to pull over, which he did. The boys noticed a tow truck parked next to the police cycle but thought nothing of it. The cop started his rant again, "You drunk, you drunk. Get out of car! We tow you." Kelly and Rob capitulated with his demands and stood next to the RX7. Immediately the tow truck driver began hitching up the beautiful new Mazda to take it away.

Kelly said to the cop, "What are you doing? Where is my car going?" The Huda replied, "Tijuana police yard. You pick up tomorrow." Rob was more pissed than Kelly and yelled out, "This sucks!" About this time the tow truck left with the rental car. The cop got on his bike and motored away leaving the boys with their mouths literally open and agape. The two-mile walk back to Skip and Billy began in the late afternoon sun.

Upon arriving at the house trailer, Kelly explained the situation to Skip and Billy. Skip's immediate response was, "It's a rental car. Forget about it. The rental company will take care of it once the TJ police notify them." Kelly didn't like this approach at first, but he started coming around to the idea, thinking he would explain it to the rental company when got back across the border.

The next day was spent relaxing with Rob and Kelly taking solo parasail rides while being pulled by a boat off the Pacific beach. The ride consisting of a standing take off from the beach and then going into the air at least a hundred feet. The boat circled around on the water and then dropped the boys back onto the sandy beach. The Mexican handler on the beach shouted, "Pull it! Pull it!" over and over again in reference to an overhead rope with a handle on it. Pulling the rope lowered the rider to the beach where the handler disconnected the parachute from Kelly or Rob as they made their individual rides. Exhilarating!

The more Kelly thought about the rental car, the less he thought about explaining it to the rental company on return to the US. He could see himself saying, "Yeah, we were drinking all afternoon and a Mexican cop pulled us over for driving under the influence. Then he towed our car away." Not much of an argument. Plus the four of them now had only one car with two seats. How would Kelly and Rob get back to the San Diego airport? Billy came up with a third option.

Billy knew a lot of locals in and around Puerto Nuevo. He knew a certain Mexican fellow who could get in and out of the States with his questionable paperwork. The name for this person was Coyote Carlos. Of course Kelly and Rob had their US IDs available if questioned at the border. If Carlos didn't make it across the border, Kelly and Rob would walk across and hail a cab to San Diego. Cabs were plentiful, sitting and waiting on the US side of the border. There were scores of Americans who had walked across the border and drank too much on Avenida Revolucion in TJ. They needed taxi rides back home. The boys were short on cash funds for Carlos, but Kelly had an emergency credit card to pay him once they were back in the States. This was now the plan, a hundred dollars each plus gas money.

The plan worked like silk after waiting for two hours at the US Border Patrol crossing. The station wagon with Mexican plates rolled up to the Border Officer who asked each of the three for ID. A quick look at the docs and they were waved into the good ole US of A. What a relief!

After a quick stop at the Bank of America, Carlos dropped the boys off at the airport and waved Adios! Kelly went straight to the car rental counter and told the attendant that their rental car was stolen from them in Mexico. The rental attendant was brusque and rude, but documented the event, stating that Kelly would be responsible for the car until it was returned. Kelly knew he would be far away in another state when the TJ police called the agency to come pick up their rental car.

The boys flew back to Florida from San Diego with the relief of being home, but having a wild story to tell as well. You stay classy, San Diego.

Chapter 8
Springtime in Tallytown

Holding back your hair has been one of my great honors.

R ob and Kelly went back to their respective schools after one adventurous spring break. The tale has been told many times verbally but never in writing.

After freezing to death in a house with no central hearing for three months, Kelly promised himself that he would not stay another quarter in the frat house. Between the drunken brother constantly coming in late at night, yelling up the stairs for those in bed to come party with him on a school night, to catching meningitis, living in that situation was not for Kelly.

Patrick had been living in the house for a while and wanted to spend more time with his girlfriend, soon to be fiancé. Patrick had found a two-bedroom apartment across campus, where he needed a roommate for the second bedroom. Kelly put his name out there with conviction! It was a done deal. Done deals sometimes come with loose ends. The Vice Archon Kevin, who also drunkenly yelled up the stairs late at night, told Kelly that he had signed up for frat house occupancy through the end of the school year. Kelly explained to Kevin that he was moving to prevent any sickness caused by an unclean house and potential contagion spreaders. Kevin was unconvinced and added Kelly's name to the posted list of brothers who owed money to the fraternity. Kelly went ahead and moved into the apartment with Patrick, ignoring the financial listing posted so that all brothers and house visitors were able to see and judge the delinquents. After his experience with meningitis and other flulike episodes,

Kelly decided to try some healthier living. It was much easier in the warmth of springtime and having your own living quarters outside of the frat house. Even though his six-foot, 150-pound frame looked thin and somewhat healthy, Kelly decided to become a neighborhood jogger. His jogs were often shirtless, as it was becoming much warmer with the associated humidity of the South. One shirtless day, Kelly took his usual street route run when a call came from an open car full of undergrads, "Hey, who let the bird out of the cage?" With that Kelly reduced the jogging; besides it was getting too hot. Kelly's physique didn't change no matter what he ate or how he exercised anyway.

Kelly continued his visits to the house on weekends, playing foosball and flirting with Gloria while her boyfriend hung out with his newly found brotherhood. Jimbo, as Kelly called him behind his back, continued to ignore Gloria at these gatherings, so Kelly stepped up.

One Saturday night Gloria had way too much to drink and was in obvious distress. Kelly escorted her into the one downstairs bathroom. It was outfitted with a single toilet but no shower. That toilet got all the use during parties and was in sad shape that late evening. But Gloria needed to let loose and Kelly was there for her. Kelly closed the bathroom door while Gloria kneeled before the urine-splattered toilet and started to lurch. Kelly delicately held back Gloria's hair while she vomited the excess ethanol she had consumed that night. The stomach contractions eventually stopped and Gloria turned and hugged Kelly. The mess was still on her mouth but Kelly held her anyway. After a while she let go, and Kelly wiped and cleaned off her mouth.

Kelly held Gloria tightly while they walked out of the bathroom, so she could go to Jimbo. When Jimbo saw what was going on he said, "I don't need this mess." With that Kelly offered, "I can drive Gloria home." Jimbo responded, "Go ahead, I got better things to do than deal with that junk." Jimbo was clearly off his rocker due to overrated masculinity and excess booze.

Kelly put his arm around Gloria's shoulder and they carefully walked out of the fraternity house. Kelly gently placed her into the passenger seat of the Pimpo (which had since been repaired from the fire). Kelly walked Gloria into her single room at the all girl's dormitory. Kelly laid Gloria down onto her single bed and massaged her perfect hair while she went to sleep. Kelly left Jennie Murphree Hall and went back to his new apartment. It was great because he didn't have to wake up a roommate when he came in late.

The next morning Kelly called Gloria's dorm room to inquire about her state. It was a slow Sunday morning, and Gloria was measured in her responses about the evening before. She told Kelly that she didn't remember a whole lot. The one thing that she vividly remembered was the care Kelly took in holding back her hair. That event became their bond as they began to date.

The next day Gloria formally broke up with Jimbo. He was livid and hateful toward Gloria and now toward Kelly. Gloria was up for election into the chapter as a little sister. The vote took place one Sunday afternoon during the weekly fraternal meeting. Jimbo had forged a faction to deny Gloria the honor of being a little sister. The group voted against her which was highly unusual. When the vote was announced by David the Archon, Kelly was furious and yelled at the chapter brothers, "You all should be the ones to have to tell her!" Kelly then stormed out of the house and would only return on very rare events for the rest of his undergraduate tenure.

Kelly and Gloria became very close, bonded, and only dated each other. Gloria would visit Kelly at his apartment, but Kelly couldn't visit much at the all-girls dormitory. One afternoon the apartment was empty except for the new couple. Kelly and Gloria lounged on Kelly's bed for a while, embracing and kissing. Kelly had an idea. He suggested to Gloria, "Let's go check out

Patrick's waterbed. He won't be home for a while." The two continued their horsing around on the waterbed, which created a whole new atmosphere and experience. The warm springtime led to short shorts and cut-off shirts. Hands went to readily accessible private parts while the breathing became heavier. Finally she said, "Play with it." Kelly had previous experience with only one other girl, Dana, and this was never one of her requests. Kelly figured out there was a certain spot that created a better response than any other. Kelly was introduced to 'Delores' and that was the key to what happened next. Kelly wasn't aware of this occurring with Dana, but Gloria had a reaction that he had never created before, the female climax. Happy returns were handily performed by Gloria for Kelly. God's in his heaven and all was right in the world.

Kelly and Gloria continued their dating which usually ended up in the same scenario as described above. It turned out that Gloria had maintained her virginity through high school and now college. She was a semi-practicing Catholic which demanded abstinence until marriage. In addition the church did not allow birth control which happened to be readily available at the college dispensary for free. Gloria was steadfast in her stance and would not allow Kelly to "go all the way." Even playing the Raspberry's song didn't help!

Chapter 9

A Summertime of Work and Good Times

Déjà vu all over again, again, and again...

K elly maintained his good GPA after the spring quarter and was making plans for a school-less summer. He was notified by his Dad that WDW had called offering him a summer job back in the food and beverage arena. Kelly accepted the summer job offer and decided to move back to the Cloud City. Good thing he had torn up that "Do not rehire" letter upon leaving last summer. The final costume was returned at the laundry room, but no letter of permanent separation was submitted.

Kelly and Gloria would take a break over the summer. She would work in a Tampa Bay hospital and he would go back to work with the mouse at Walt's place. They couldn't really get together since she had weekends off, but weekends were the busy time at WDW. Kelly got midweek days off.

Even though Kelly would be living in the Cloud City for the summer, he had no intentions of living back home. Kelly and Tuck made plans to rent a two-bedroom furnished apartment in the Cloud City. Tuck would go back to the Methodist Church to make some money for college. Kelly left first and arranged the lease at the Montana Avenue Apartments.

Tuck called Kelly up with the bad news: He wasn't coming home. The church position had fallen through, so he decided to stay in Tally. "Crap! What am I going to do now?" thought Kelly. "All my money is going to be spent on this place and I won't have any money for tuition next fall." Kelly had signed a lease for the next three months and was stuck. Tuck wasn't even attending school. Where was his money coming from? Tuck hinted that he had a trust from his passed parents. Tuck had bigger ambitions too. He wanted to become the head of the PiPhi chapter, the archon.

Kelly fell into the routine of work, coming home to his empty two-bedroom apartment, and going back to work. Kelly heard that one of his high school friends was back in town for the summer. Hyman had gone to the Army Academy for his first year of college and now had the summer off. Rob and Kelly had actually driven Hyman to the MCO airport for his trip to West Point the previous year. Kelly contacted Hyman and they decided to room together. Hyman took a lot of grief for his name, but Kelly was sure it made him a stronger person. Thank god the rent could get paid now, with some money left over for the fall semester.

Kelly noticed a group of four younger girls across the way in a lower level apartment. Upon introducing himself it was coincidental but Kelly and the girls all worked at WDW. The girls were from South Florida and had taken temporary summer jobs as dancers and entertainers at the amusement park. They all attended the same dance school at home during the school year. They were on their own with no parents or adult chaperons living with them even though they were still 16-18 year old high schoolers or recent graduates.

The ones who befriended Kelly were Becky, 16, Audrey, 17, and Lydia, 18. All the girls had attachments back home, but were now on their own for three months. Kelly spent time in their apartment, but Kelly's place was the party house, much to the chagrin of the downstairs neighbors. KISS music and other rock bands of the late '70s blared from Kelly's stereo most every night, and the girls would come over.

The downstairs neighbor, Scott, was a car and motorcycle mechanic who had a morning job requiring normal sleep hours.

He never really complained until Kelly's old friend Curt came over with the latest beer trick. Curt would stand on the stairwell after drinking half his bottle of beer. The stunt was to smash your palm over the opening of the half-filled bottle causing the glass bottom of the bottle to fly off and crash onto the stairwell and patio below. The next morning the outside stairs and Scott's concrete entrance was covered in glass. Kelly had to go to work that morning, so the glass didn't get cleaned up. Scott was miffed about this transgression, but a Fourth of July escapade upset him even more.

One or more of Kelly's partygoer friends had fireworks that night. Scott had a vintage red Stingray in the parking lot that was usually covered with a car cover, but was bare this night. The fireworks got set off in the parking lot either near or on Scott's perfect Corvette Stingray. Kelly got the blame, but he insisted it was not him and it was one of the other guys. That didn't matter to Scott since it was Kelly's contingency. It's a small world but Scott became a good friend to Kelly Sr. later in life. Kelly Jr. would have to hear the fireworks transgression story every time he went home to visit his dad and Scott was around.

So Skip got a leave from the Army and travelled back to the Cloud City. He ended up spending most of his time at Kelly's apartment and not so much with Mom and Dad. However, there was a routine Sunday night dinner at the family house on Ohio Avenue.

Skip met the neighbor girls and took a liking to Becky. Becky was blondish, young and sensual. Skip and Becky would disappear sometimes into Becky's room during get-togethers at the girls' place. When it was time for Skip to go back to Texas and perform his military duties, he was very reluctant to leave. Lo and behold a week later, Skip showed up at the Montana Street apartments again. Skip said, "I told my CO that my girlfriend was having a baby and I had to go home." Skip got a leave of absence to hang out and date Becky for the next three weeks.

Kelly liked Audrey. Audrey had light brown hair and was nicely voluptuous. Kelly would sit with Audrey at all the parties. One time they were alone sitting on the bed, kissing in Kelly's room. Kelly asked Audrey, "Do you want me to turn off the light?" Audrey got uncomfortable and began squirming away from Kelly, probably thinking of her boyfriend back home. The two rejoined the group out in Kelly's living room. Lydia was observing Kelly and Audrey, glaring with the stink-eye.

Lydia had light brown skin with dark hair and was of Latin heritage. That meant Cuban during those days in Florida. It turned out that Lydia had a thing for Kelly, and Audrey was taking Kelly away. Dear reader, is this starting to sound familiar? It was another triangle whereby so and so likes that one, but the third one likes so and so. This event also happened during Kelly's high school days with Hanna and Debra. Kelly was starting to feel cursed. Maybe it was a good thing since he didn't end up cheating on Gloria.

Kelly felt rejected by Audrey so the house parties began to fall off. Skip went back to his Army gig in Texas. Kelly went to work five days a week and came home to a quiet apartment. One evening Audrey knocked on the door and asked Kelly from the doorway, "Do you have our ice cube trays?" Kelly responded "No" and closed the door. Later on, thinking about the encounter, Kelly realized that based on her docile tone, Audrey may have wanted to make amends and be friends again. It didn't happen and the two apartments remained mostly separate. A few hand waves and hellos here and there, but nothing much more than that.

One afternoon off, Kelly had a few drinks while listening to KISS *Alive II*. He decided to walk across to where the girls lived. Outside their door was an empty cork board for posting advertisements or messages about lost pets. Kelly somehow decided to tear the corkboard off the wall and toss it out into the grass by the pool. Lydia came out and said in a quiet voice, "Kelly, what's going on?" Kelly didn't really have an answer since he felt a number of emotions, including frustration, happiness, loneliness, and a mild buzz all at the same time. Unfortunately, the complex manager happened to be at the pool and observed the whole incident. The next day, Kelly received a call from the apartment office that part of his deposit would have to be used to replace the corkboard. "Scheisse! I am a Scheissekopf," Kelly said to himself after hanging up the phone.

The rest of the summer was uneventful. Hyman had gone back to Army school toward the end of August. Kelly checked out of WDW on August 31 without the "no rehire" notification to the laundry management this time. Why the checkout documentation was entrusted to the employee and the laundry, Kelly would never know.

He drove back to the Cloud City from WDW, packed his few things into the Pimpo and headed for Grandma's house in South Florida. School didn't start until late September, so Kelly had time to enjoy the fare coming from Grandma's kitchen for a little while.

Grandma went grocery shopping almost every morning to buy the southern nourishment served up for dinner (which was really lunch). At supper time Grandma would make Grandpa, Uncle George, and Kelly a simple sandwich of their choosing. One night Kelly chose a chicken sandwich from the left over "dinner" chicken. Grandma would lather the bread with mayonnaise, apply the chicken, and bring the plates out to the large dining room table. There were never any paper plates, and all meals were served with metal cutlery and china. One night Kelly began to feel crunching in his sandwich and spit out the chewed up sandwich. There were glass shards in his rejected spittle, but nothing in his mouth had been cut. Luckily, he hadn't swallowed any of the insalubrious mouth mix.

Kelly asked Grandma, "What happened to my sandwich? There's broken glass in it!" Grandma sheepishly admitted that she had dropped and shattered the mayonnaise jar on the kitchen floor. "I didn't want to waste any mayo, so I scooped some of it up." She was apologetic at first, but later it seemed to be a non-issue for her. The occurrence was forgotten as it seemed like water off a duck's back to Grandma. Kelly didn't complain as he knew his grandparents had suffered the Great Depression.

Grandma had a built-in kitchen dishwasher provided by Kelly's dad, but she never used it. All dishes and silverware were washed by hand. That mimicked the unused clothes dryer in the laundry room. All wet clothing was dried on a clothes hanger in the back yard. Kelly was not sure how they dried in that 95 percent humidity, but they did. Maybe the yard flowers made the clothes smell better since no dryer sheets were used. Come to think of it, there was no such thing as dryer sheets back then.

Kelly asked Grandma, "Why do you call the refrigerator an ice box?" She replied in her South Georgia drawl, "Cuz that's what it is." Kelly didn't argue even though everyone knew the iceman didn't show up every morning anymore.

Kelly packed up the Pimpo for another ride back to North Florida, leaving Grandma's house. Grandma didn't show her emotion, but Kelly knew she had a special place in her heart for him. Grandma felt bad about all the up and down emotions that Kelly and his sister Kathy had had to endure during their early lives. In a loving gesture that Kelly could never repay, Kelly's grandma restarted her checks for Kelly's tuition. School was back in session. Grandma's checks were identical to his college attendance. If Kelly was out for the summer, the checks would correctly stop coming. Kelly was forever in her debt, as his dad and mother did not contribute a penny for the remainder of his college career.

Chapter 10
A Living Space with Stability

Fruition to freedom comes in stepwise fashion.
Wait, are we ever really free?

Unexpectedly, the apartment above the one Kelly had shared with Patrick in the spring had come open. Kelly and his pledge brother Herbert jumped at the opportunity. There was a pledger to the fraternity from the previous winter who was also interested. Johnboy, as he was called, even to his face, wanted to move out of his parents' home in the affluent, golf course part of Tallytown. It was never clear to Kelly if Johnboy's parents wanted him out, or if Johnboy wanted his independence. After living with Johnboy a while it was clear what was going on. Johnboy was a self-centered only child whose parents wanted him to gain some individuality and understanding of the real world. Johnboy's dad even once sidled up to Kelly at some gathering or another, and asked Kelly to watch over his son. Kelly promised to try, but it became a real hit and miss task.

At the beginning, Herbert spent 80 percent of his time on his university studies and 20 percent working at Albertson's grocery store. Over the next year or so, he would flip the percentages to 80 percent Albertson's and 20 percent schooling. During Kelly's junior year Herbert spent 100 percent of his outside time performing grocery management and dropped out of school. As long as the rent money kept coming, Kelly was OK with it. It was Herbert's decision in life to make. Herbert was really good with people, as Kelly observed in one of his visits to the store. Herbert was in his element directing and helping customers in his very accommodating but lispy fashion.

The apartment had a master bedroom with its own shower/bathtub and toilet. The second bedroom had a shared second bathroom with the third roommate and visitors. The dining room was in the back of the apartment down the hall and behind the kitchen. The dining room was easily convertible to a third bedroom by adding a sliding door to its entrance. This would be Herbert's room with an understanding by all roommates that they would rotate the rooms each quarter. Johnboy got the second bedroom and Kelly occupied the master bedroom.

Kelly and Gloria reignited their relationship. Both were afraid their separation over the summer would be the end. With only a single visit to Gloria's house in the Tampa Bay area during the summer and minimal phone calls, the bond could have easily been broken. But it wasn't. Things picked up right where they left off with Gloria back in her girls' dormitory and the two spending a lot of time in Kelly's apartment room. Kelly had a large king size bed and a black and white TV for lounging around. Going all the way was still verboten, but pleasurable events were still enjoyed. Kelly continued to push Gloria to visit the campus clinic for birth control, but the idea was nevertheless rejected by Gloria. By the end of the fall quarter, Kelly selfishly made it clear that if things didn't progress the two would likely go their separate ways. Gloria resisted the notion less and less over time and seemed resigned to the eventual outcome.

Johnboy turned out to be a real piece of work. He was about six feet two, 130 pounds, with eyes of blue and curly perm-like dark hair. He spent long periods coiffing in the bathroom each morning before class and then running down the stairs to his waiting red Chevy Camaro. After checking his look in the rear view mirror *and* the side mirror he drove off to class. Kelly had no idea where Johnboy found parking on campus, but he always drove the Camaro.

Kelly either walked to his classes on the west side of campus or rode his bicycle if the class was on the east side. Usually liberal arts classes like Old Testament History or English Composition were up 10th gear bicycle hills on the east side, or science courses on the west side. Since Kelly was a science major, more and more classes were within walking distance of his apartment.

Kelly maintained his daily attendance to classes and evening trips to the library for test preparation or homework. In the evening there was plenty of parking outside the library, so he took his car. Gloria and Kelly would meet up for a quiet study session and between reading books on calculus and chemistry, read the graffiti inked or scratched onto the large, white, wooden tables. Kelly's favorite study spot had the lyrics to Pink Floyd's "Money" etched onto the table. These lyrics were dreams for Kelly of his future potential, especially references to obtaining a good job with good pay.

One Saturday night Kelly and Gloria dressed up in more than their normal shorts and t-shirts to go out for dinner. It was Gloria's birthday so they decided to go to a semi-fancy fondue restaurant. The low lounge chairs in the darkened dining room with pieces of cooked meat on the grill led to date feeding. Date feeding led to dangling pieces of meat above each other's mouths and much giggling. Not much nutrition was received that night, but a good time was had by both!

In Kelly's POS after the fondue experience, Kelly asked Gloria if she wanted to stop by the frat house. She thought for a minute and the said, "OK, we shouldn't stay long." The two hadn't been to the house in weeks, but upon walking in the front door were roundly greeted. Was it sincere or was it the consumed beer welcoming them? No matter, the two went to the kitchen where Kelly drew two beers from the keg. Greg and Patrick were hunched over the foosball table playing individually. Patrick was kicking Greg's butt as evidenced by the amount of score rings above his goal hole. Patrick had a knack for offensively moving his front foosmen to shuffle the white ball in front of his opponent's goal. He could control the ball, back and forth, before whacking the ball into the poorly guarded goal.

Greg and Patrick excitedly asked Kelly and Gloria to play doubles. It was clear that their solo game was over. Kelly and Gloria accepted, and were roundly defeated. Even though Kelly's defensive skills were good, they were no match for Patrick's offensive skills. The game was over and the couple moved to the living room to say long-overdue hellos and catch up conversations with some of the brothers such as Tuck, Harrison, David, Greg, and Patrick. Patrick always wanted to be Kelly's big brother, since Greg had a number of other little brothers. Even over the years Patrick would contact Kelly to update him on reunions or other events. Kelly never attended any since he had been a bit blackballed by the Chapter. Jimbo and his cronies hung out separately and never said hi, hello, or how are you? Maybe it was better that way, Kelly reflected, on their way back to his place.

Sunday mornings usually invited a late awakening from a slumber that started in the wee hours. Sunday was a lazy day for hanging around the complex pool, watching football, or listening to music. Sunday night required a visit to the library in preparation for the upcoming week.

Kelly was a huge rock music fan and his LP collection had grown considerably due to a cheap record store on Tennessee Street known, strangely enough, as College Records. The record store was visited once a week, usually on Friday afternoons for a single LP purchase. Kelly's friend Geoff from across the hall was big into music also. The two would usually accompany each other on the record buying trip. Upon returning home, the illustrated record covers had their cellophane sheets removed and the vinyl was placed onto one of the neighbor's turntables. Beer would flow, blood would spill, and a good time was had by all. Well, everything except the blood spilling.

Chapter 11
The Moment of Truth

We are mysterious creatures and in the end most of it doesn't matter.
So live while you can, the rest is water over the dam.

K elly still got together with some of his fraternity friends. Harrison loved to play pool or pinball, so Henry's Bar was good for those. The bar, even though a dump, was patronized by upscale fraternity brothers and rich sorority girls. Kelly never understood the attraction of these people to a dive bar, but there it was. Gloria had gone home for the weekend which she did occasionally, as she was close to her family. Gloria drove her 1972 white Cutlass fastback to Clearwater and back on these weekends. Kelly would get the boys around and do some celebrating on these Fridays and Saturdays.

One Saturday afternoon, Harrison and Geoff joined Kelly for some pinball and billiards at Henry's. Beers were sipped, rum was shot, and cigars were brought out. Smoking in bars was fine back then. After a few puffs on his gifted cigar, Kelly was feeling a little nauseous, and then he was feeling very nauseous. He ran to the swinging front door and let out a gusher that would have made any bar drinker proud. Unfortunately, at that very same time three sorority sisters were entering dressed in their fancy dresses and slip on shoes with bows over the toes. Kelly remembered the girls' shoes because that's all he saw as he leaned over. Chunks were spewed while the girls screamed, "EEEWWW!" Kelly hustled to the parking lot, got in his car, and raced home before the sorority sisters' boyfriends could find him.

The rest of the fall quarter was spent studying hard, partying hard, and spending time with Gloria. In December when finals were starting and the quarter was wrapping up, Gloria had a surprise for Kelly. She had obtained birth control pills from the campus clinic and had begun taking the little white tablets. Kelly said, "So, we're good to go!" "Not so fast slugger," Gloria replied to his come-on, with the following,"I need a whole month of the pill before I am safe." "Aw jeez, that puts us out 'til after the New Year," Kelly whined. "Take it or leave it," Gloria replied with the authority and the power of the situation. As it should be.

Kelly and Gloria departed ways for the holiday to be with their respective families. Kelly couldn't wait to get back in January for their long awaited tryst.

But before Kelly could drive home for Christmas, he had to get the Pimpo running. Over the years the Pimpo was notorious for having a failing battery to go along with its failing starter. Luckily Geoff from across the hall had not yet left for his holiday leave. Kelly rousted Geoff from his late morning sleep and asked him for help get the POS running. Kelly had heard that if a car had a manual transmission, it could be started without a viable battery. Geoff confirmed that theory.

The two trudged down the stairs and into the parking lot to deal with a dead 'horse'. Kelly and Geoff moved the Pinto out onto a straightaway of the parking lot. Geoff got behind the car doing all the push work, while Kelly sat behind the wheel with the clutch engaged and the car in second gear. After three attempts of pushing the car to about ten mph and 'popping the clutch', there was no reaction from the engine. Geoff was gassed and ready to pass out by this time. He had had a heavy night the previous evening. Geoff said, "Let's trade spots." Kelly agreed and moved to the rear bumper. Geoff sat down in the driver's seat, and angrily berated Kelly, "You didn't have the key turned on!" One quick push, one popped clutch and the Pimpo roared to life. Geoff put it in neutral, got out, trading places with Kelly. Kelly couldn't turn off the ignition, so he waved goodbye to Geoff out the driver's window and headed home. Kelly didn't turn the car off for the entire 250-mile drive, even while filling the tank with gas. Law, what law?

The holidays in Cloud City were uneventful. Kelly stayed with his dad and mom in the ranch house on Ohio Avenue. Kelly popped in and out of his adolescent home to visit his high school buddies, now returned from their distant schools. Rob and Rog were back visiting in their respective parents' homes. Al threw his recurring nighttime party in the woods by Lake Hope. The ex-high schoolers gathered around the fire, sipping their drink of choice.

Kelly mostly conversed with the guys about old times. "Hey, do you remember when this happened? Hey, do you remember when that happened?" Every time Kelly saw Curt at a get-together or reunion over future years, it would be, "Hey Curt, do you remember that time I kneed you in the balls?" Curt would always reluctantly reply, "Yeah, I remember." Nothing further was said or needed to be said. It was pretty much the same with everyone's discussions about past youthful occurrences. Questions were posed to others about what they were up to now, but no one really cared, and those conversations ended quickly.

Kelly thought he saw Gabby in the shadows across the fire. Kelly and Gabby were high school lunch line buddies. Kelly would point out to Gabby what was a good dish made by the hair-netted octogenarians and what wasn't. This was about as far as they had socialized in high school since Kelly didn't want any ties to the Cloud City and Gabby was a year younger. But now was different. Gabby had transformed into a striking young woman, and Kelly knew she had always had an eye for him.

Kelly took the familiar long walk over to the waiting girl. She was glad to see him and he was glad to see her. Kelly inquired, "Would you like to take a walk?" The answer was "yes" and the two walked out toward the main road. Kelly's Pinto was parked in the dark with no one around. "Would you like to sit in the car?" The answer was "yes." Kelly felt tingles of electricity when he looked across the dark car at Gabby. Any thoughts of Gloria were nowhere near his consciousness. Guys have this infirmity where their brain sometimes sinks way below their cranium.

The two looked toward each other, inches apart, and Kelly placed a light kiss on Gabby's lips. The encounter proceeded to hugging and French kissing as both had imagined since high school. This went on for a while and Kelly made the next move. "Would you like to go to the backseat?" Gabby replied with an emphatic "No." This was probably for the best and the fleeting couple went back to the party. The two never saw each other again after this lovely happenstance, but it will always be remembered by Kelly, and hopefully by Gabby.

Rog and Kelly again had to drive Rob home after his annual meeting with Mr. Southern Comfort. The three piled into the Pimpo with Rob's head hanging out the open passenger window in case of an accidental loss of his dinner or other consumed solids and liquids. The next morning Kelly's dad asked him, "What is that stain all over the passenger door of your car?" Of course he knew full well what it was. The apple don't fall too far from the tree.

Kelly drove back to school in great anticipation of the 'moment of truth' with Gloria. In fact Gloria came over that night to the apartment. Gloria announced, "We have two more weeks to go! I started the contra pills in mid-December." Kelly's positive spirits and his aching groin were devastated. "I thought you started at the beginning of December? Arggggggh!" The waiting game began again.

The night of reckoning had come. The normal foreplay began on Kelly's king size bed. Gloria was obviously inexperienced at going full scale, not that Kelly had tons of know-how, being with only one other girl. Gloria froze and lay there like a dead dog. Kelly encouraged her by saying, "You know it will be better if we both move." The action was completed, and the relief was profound for both. Kelly had become one with his lover and

Gloria had completed a huge step between her adolescence and her adulthood. But where would this lead them in the future? How would it affect them going forward? These questions have been asked throughout the ages of humankind, but they were brand new for this couple.

Chapter 12
Professors

From the first butt slap and cry, we must learn to comply.

B y now Kelly had been exposed to many types of professors. Some were standoffish and brash. Some were open and benevolent. Some started out as brazen, but when a one-on-one meeting occurred, the teacher became more understanding and personable.

Kelly also noted that the younger female professors smiled in his presence and acted kindly towards him. At the start of Kelly's third semester in English writing, Dr. Blossom was distant with the students. Kelly was receiving Cs on his papers and this was unacceptable for his GPA. He decided to make a visit during office hours. Dr. Blossom was negative and detached at first. "What do you want?" she started. However, after a few minutes she began to warm up. Then it was, "How can I help you?" Kelly wasn't sure if it was his mannerisms, his personality, or his looks, but it worked. Maybe it was a combination of all. . Anyway, after that meeting Kelly began receiving As on all his papers and smiles in the classroom.

One thing Kelly learned early on was to make sure his work perfectly matched the desires of the professor. What they wrote on the blackboard (yes, blackboard) or put in the syllabus was to be followed to a T. Kelly had wanted to use his own mind, thoughts, and approaches to the assignments but quickly found out that approach was doomed to failure. Mimicking exactly was the prof wanted got the Agrade. Kelly pulled out his psychology card and concluded that this approach fueled the ego of the teacher so he gladly complied. Both parties got what they wanted.

Kelly's Spanish III professor was also a younger female. She fell into the category of instantly friendly and helpful. Dr. Flora had previously been Kelly's professor of Spanish I during the time he had been hospitalized and had missed two weeks from meningitis. She had been very understanding then and was helpful getting Kelly back on track after his absence. Dr. Flora was young, Latin, and full of energy. She bopped around the classroom individually checking students for their Spanish speaking prowess. She seemed to spend an unequal amount of time in front of Kelly ensuring his knowledge of the subjective case and other nuances of Castilian Spanish. There seemed to be more than that under the surface, but Kelly wasn't going to go there. He ensured his work was perfectly molded to the professor's requests and he achieved an A+. Kelly sometimes fantasized if that would also be his grade in other activities with Dr. Flora, but he would never go down that track.

Then there were the a**hole professors. Dr. Richard Peters was Kelly's organic chemistry professor. Dr. Peters had been around so long, that he had taught chemistry to Kelly's dad, Kelly Sr. Kelly Sr. said that Dr. Peters had been a jerk even during his time twenty years earlier. Kelly Sr. flunked his first go-around with organic chemistry under Dr. Peters. He had to retake the class to obtain a much-improved A.

Organic chemistry was known to be a "weed out" class for all the med school wannabes. Around 90 percent did fail organic and moved on the other majors rather than Pre-Med. The lectures were totally unhelpful and the professor interaction with the class was non-existent. One blackboard was filled with chalk drawings, to be rolled up for students to copy, while the bottom board was filled with carbon reactions that the students were to copy and learn. Then the boards were flipped and the formerly upper board was erased and replaced with more organically uninteresting permutations and transformations.

But these equations had to be learned to pass the weekly tests, the mid-term, and the final. The thing Kelly first observed after flunking the first weekly test was that the test questions and required formulations were from the book questions at the end of each chapter in Morrison and Boyd's *Organic Chemistry*. Rarely were the test questions drawn from any information presented three times a week in classes. Some would call it laziness to create a test using pre-printed questions in the textbook. However, Kelly wasn't complaining because after discovering this bit of knowledge, his overall grade began improving. Of course all good things come to an end.

It was time for the mid-term exam which constituted 25 percent of the overall grade. "Oh hell no!" Kelly muttered upon receiving the blank mimeographed exam. These questions were not from the bookchapter questions. . Kelly floundered and made up the best formulary reactions he could, but to no avail. He received a big fat D on the mid-term. "There goes my medical school admission," Kelly lamented. Kelly found one of his answers on the mid-term that he felt was correct and decided to visit Dr. Peters in his office. If corrected his grade would rise to at least a C. It was the first time Kelly didn't have to wait outside a professor's door during their office hours. He walked right into the office that contained a sour face and few words.

"Yes?" was the acrid question from the scouring face. "I think I had the correct answer on one of the mid-term questions." Kelly put the paper down before Dr. Peters. The professor reluctantly picked it up and looked. The answers had been written in pencil and this one had obviously been erased and replaced. "You changed the answer," charged the professor. Kelly replied, "Yes, I did but it was during the test." Dr. Peters sneered, but grudgingly changed the grade.

Kelly vowed to never have to make that office visit again. He would study Organic as much and as hard as he could. The only problem was that Organic Chemistry was very different from any other class he had ever had. There was no memorization involved. It was more of a way of thinking that would create new found carbon reactions from those learned in class or from Morrison and Boyd. These new reactions were requested as test answers. "Arrrgg!" Kelly exclaimed upon this realization.

Kelly earned Cs in his first two quarters of Organic Chemistry, but improved to a B in the third quarter. He hoped this would help his argument during interviews for medical school. Kelly knew that Cs were landmines for achieving his major, major goal.

Chapter 13

Girlfriends, Semi-Girlfriends and Passers in the Night

The workers will play when the boss is away.

Kelly and Gloria maintained their amorous relationship through the winter and into the spring months. All was right as each could express themselves with no hindrances. Gloria seemed relieved that she had a weight off of her back, and Kelly was relieved that he didn't have to bug Gloria anymore about something they disagreed on.

Gloria was driven to a professional career and Kelly shared similar long-term desires and goals. They both studied hard through the winter months and were relieved when the sunny spring days emerged. Kelly and Gloria were both from more southern regions of the state that didn't have winters as cold as those in the panhandle. They could now study at the pool that was just below Kelly's apartment. Gloria was much lighter skinned than Kelly due to her reddish hair and northern European heritage. Kelly always told Gloria that she was so fair skinned because peoples from northern climates needed to absorb the sun's vitamin D more quickly than those in southern regions.

This desire to relax or study for longer periods in the sun occasionally created an argument. When Gloria began to turn red, she stood up and announced, "I'm going upstairs." Kelly would be miffed because he was just beginning to get a decent tan. It soon became a chink in their armor, but was not a huge issue. Gloria was a mellow person and rarely had disagreements with Kelly. Was it becoming too easy with no challenges?

Late that spring Gloria prepared for her internship down in Clearwater. Kelly decided to stay and take classes in the scantly (and scantily clad) populated summer quarter. A pre-med required more hours to graduate than other degrees, so this summer term was very helpful to Kelly. Johnboy was also taking a few classes during the summer and Herbert was now working full time at Albertson's. Rent money was not an issue as plenty was available from Johnboy's rich parents and Herbert's sixty-hour-a-week job. Grandma came through, helping Kelly even though it was summertime. The electric bill was divided by three. Each phone call on the phone bill was separated by caller and added up. There was no overall phone bill back in those days. Long distance calls were especially expensive.

The roommates had not followed through on their agreement to rotate bedrooms each quarter, although Kelly continued to pay more for the master bedroom. Herbert was tired of his sliding curtain-type door separation and could now afford his own one-bedroom closer to work. He announced that he would be leaving at the end of the summer.

Gloria asked Kelly if she could leave her belongings in his double wide closet for the summer and he agreed. This created an unstated mental bond between the two until they were back together. Maybe that was part of Gloria's strategy. Three months was a long time and Kelly started to notice the girls around campus and certainly the girls around the apartment pool.

Kelly had a lighter than normal load during the summer, but twelve hours was still considered a full load. So he had time to hang out at the pool, go visit his remaining buddies at the frat house, and think about a potential rendezvous with a female classmate, a poolgoer, a frat party attendee, or a bar visitor. Conversations were had with many of these girls but nothing transpired as he was still involved with Gloria.

Kelly would go to Ken's Bar with his buds Geoff and Harrison. Kelly would be playing the KISS pinball machine and a pretty blonde would saunter over to talk to him. Kelly thought, "Is she tipsy or am I attractive to the opposite sex?" Maybe some of both.

Kelly didn't like rejection, so he rarely put his foot forward to talk with the college girls. Sometimes a bit of courage could be imbibed to help in these situations. For example, one night at the fraternity, an unknown, thin blonde was very friendly. Kelly had the bright idea to do some night swimming back at his pool. She agreed and off they went. Kelly didn't even know her name. Maybe that was part of the attraction. They had to stop by her dorm and pick up her swimsuit. They changed back at Kelly's place and slipped into the shallow end of the pool. The necking began on a warm summer night in a cool pool. Necking progressed to fondling. Luckily there were no other attendees in the cement pond.

The magnetism moved upstairs to Kelly's apartment room. Wet bathing suits had to be removed and the great deed ensued on Kelly's lumpy king bed. She had to get back that night, so Kelly drove her back to her room. Neither phone numbers, much less names were shared. This was highly strange for Kelly, but it was enthralling nonetheless. Oddly Kelly didn't feel much guilt as he wasn't ready to get married and felt that he may have been missing out on some part of his life.

The following Saturday, Kelly went trolling again at the frat house. There she was again, sitting on the hallway stairs. She was just as friendly and seemed just as interested. This time names were immediately exchanged. Shannon was scantily clad in the non-air conditioned house with 90-degree heat and 90 percent humidity outside. She seemed ready to get out of that hotbox and head somewhere with Kelly. That somewhere again turned out to be Kelly's pool. The darkened pool area was again vacant except for the two young love makers. This time the ultimate primal endeavor was performed in a body of clear blue water. It didn't work very well because the natural lubricants were washed away making for a rough go of it. That could be corrected upstairs, where they headed. This time the night was spent at Kelly's where sleep was a secondary verb.

Kelly took Shannon home the next morning, and sadly that was the last time they would see each other. Or was that her staring at him six months later in the Union Square? The lesson learned here was, "don't go too far too fast, if you want something to last."

One of the newer PiPhi fraternity members by the name of Joe had an apartment near Kelly's. They would sometimes see each other walking toward campus which was three blocks away. One day Joe was conversating with a young blonde. She had tightly cropped bleachy hair, however with a few extra pounds for Kelly's taste. At 5'6" with a light brown head of hair that got a lot of attention, Joe had a knack for speaking with the ladies, otherwise known as "the gift of gab." If you listened to Joe, it didn't end there either.

Kelly approached the pair and the busty blonde was introduced as Cheri. The three walked together toward campus, as each had a one o-clock class. Joe exhibited little interest in Cheri, as if he had been there, done that already. Since Joe appeared neutral to Cheri, Kelly picked up the ball and asked Cheri to lunch after class. All meals during college were later than normal so they met mid-afternoon at the Student Union Cafeteria for a normally late lunch. Cheri was very vociferous, describing herself and her experiences at school over the past year. Cheri also paid a lot of visual attention toward Kelly, peering over her glass of iced tea at him. Kelly wondered, "Is she toying with me? It seems like flirtation, but I don't want to be rejected." Kelly didn't realize during this time in his life that the female's first rejection wasn't necessarily real. There was usually some back and forth before getting to "Yes." It was the ladies' way of playing hard to get and not appearing too easy.

Since Cheri was not the best looking attraction in his life,

Kelly decided to go ahead and make an advance. "Would you like to stop by my place on your way home?" Kelly questioned Cheri. It was if she had been anticipating that question, so emphatic was her positive response. So they began the walk back, past the science buildings and the west campus dorms getting to know each other. A little bit of pinching and innocent touching occurred while they walked.

A block away from Kelly's place was a large Jax liquor store. Kelly asked, since it was Friday afternoon, "Do you want to get a bottle of wine from Jax?" It was agreed and up the slight hill they walked to procure a bottle of red Boones Farm. It was cheap wine but always did the trick.

Back at Kelly's they sat down at the table by the front window overlooking the pool and the late sunbathers. Usually the pool area thinned out when *General Hospital* came on. First the girls would leave and then the boys left, realizing they had no more eye candy.

Kelly unscrewed the wine cap and poured the wine into two glasses that were stored way up at the top of the cabinet and rarely used. The next thing Kelly realized was that the wine bottle was already empty. How did that happen so fast? Kelly guessed that he wasn't paying attention to the wine but rather to Cheri. "Let's go back to Jax for another bottle!" Kelly exclaimed. Even though the store was close neither one wanted to trudge up that hill again, so they took the Pimpo.

Another bottle of red wine was unscrewed (not uncorked) back at the apartment. This time they moved up in the world to Franzia wine at Cheri's request. Kelly didn't mind because it was still cheap.

About halfway through the second bottle there was an unstated move to Kelly's bedroom. There were no chairs, so they spread out on the bed. One thing led to another and Cheri was suddenly on top of Kelly. Clothes went flying and Cheri had her way with Kelly. It was confirmed that Cheri had a few extra chunks and a spare tire but that was definitely overlooked at this point. After a mutually satisfactory outcome, the two reclothed and went back to the unfinished bottle. Upon completing the wine, they exchanged numbers and Cheri left walking back to her nearby apartment building.

The two would never call each other or reacquaint. One time Kelly saw Cheri walking down West Call Street toward campus, but he went the other way.

There were three flaxen haired, striking girls who roomed together at Kelly's apartment complex. Two were identical twins, Mary and Carrie. However, the twins were better known to the inhabitants of the Dramedy Club Apartments as Loosey and Goosy. One twin was biblically well known to many guys around the complex. Even the plain looking Hernando bragged that he once had his way with one of the twins. No one could keep track of which was Loosey and which was Goosy. But once the party began on the deck above the pool, it became clear and the names fit perfectly. Mary (Goosy) was mostly standoffish and waddled at the gathering with her beak up in the air. Carrie (Loosey) was playful, friendly, well-oiled, and had a come-on look most of the night. She usually didn't make it to "most of the night," and left with someone or the other.

The third roommate, Sandy seemed more serious, even though she was looking to have fun. She didn't drink much and handled herself with style. Kelly liked the ones who were in the shadows of those out front giving it all they had. His theory was that the "out-fronters" would burn themselves up much too young, if not by tomorrow. But here came Carrie (Loosey) toward Kelly. She was smiling and gave him a blotto 'hello'. Carrie didn't have much more to say, and gave big smiles to Kelly. Finally Kelly said, "Do you want to take a walk?" This was becoming his come-on line. He knew he would have to come up with something better in the future.

Anyway, the 'walk' consisted of twenty-foot trip and then up the stairs to Kelly's apartment. Carrie followed without any disagreement. Once inside the apartment Carrie wanted to see Johnboy's room for some reason. Johnboy was infamous around the complex for his 130-pound frame and constantly twiddling with his hair around the pool. Carrie had carried a large cup of red punch from the party. The cup had "disaster" written all over it but Kelly didn't pay enough attention. While Carrie placed her face into Kelly's face, half the cup of punch ended up on Johnboy's bed.

Kelly was into the moment and didn't have time to clean up the mess, so the two went down the hall to Kelly's room for further activities. The remaining punch was dumped down the bathroom sink on the way and the bedroom door was locked behind them. The two sprawled onto the bed and started nature's fun and games.

Not five minutes had passed and a huge banging with yells of "KELLY!" were heard coming from his door. Kelly tried to ignore the cacophony but it was useless. The pounding continued, so Kelly got up and saw not one, but three people at the door: Johnboy, Johnboy's girlfriend Heidi, and Beau from the party. Johnboy was screaming about the punch on his bedsheets. Johnboy was very meticulous about his bedroom, clothing, and hygiene. A spill of red alcohol on his sleep escape was almost as bad as if a nuclear bomb had hit it. One time Heidi had forgotten to make Johnboy's bed before leaving for class, and it seemed that Johnboy was going to break up with her. Eventually Johnboy's small head got the better of him and he and Heidi made up.

Carrie was in an alcoholic/emotional shock at what was happening. Joe tried to console her while Kelly dealt with Johnboy's rants with promises of "I'll clean it up." Kelly escorted the dizzy, shocked, and silent Carrie back to her apartment. That night's crossing of paths was never mentioned again when Kelly saw Carrie around the complex. It was as if her alcohol content had dissolved the memory of what happened that night. On the other hand Kelly thought it might have been the shame of what had transpired.

Kelly then tried his hand with the third roommate, Sandy. The two went out to dinner one evening and then visited Fred's for rum and cokes. No lime, please. A lime takes room in the glass away from the drink. The two took a seat at a group table to enjoy their drinks. Kelly sat with his back to the wall, so that to face Kelly, Sandy had to face the wall. She wasn't happy with the setup, since she could not peruse the room. Kelly decided it was time to go. It was still early in the evening when they arrived at Sandy's apartment. Sandy invited Kelly in and he accepted. She immediately went to a container on the coffee table. A pre-rolled joint was immediately sparked up. After taking a hit, Sandy offered Kelly the funny cigarette. Kelly was anti-marijuana and he then made an excuse to leave. Sandy was not happy as it was still early in the evening. The two would not meet up again.

Kelly began to curb the female capers knowing that Gloria would be back to campus soon. In fact the summer quarter had ended and fall quarter would not start for another three weeks. What to do? Tuck had a proposal. He told Kelly, "Hey I have an old '50s Chevy that was willed to me and is sitting out in Ft. Worth. Do you want to take a road trip and bring it back?" Kelly had nothing better to do and thought they could stop and see his Aunt June and his cousins in Port Arthur. Aunt June was Kelly Sr.'s sister and had made a generous contribution toward Kelly Jr.'s tuition needs at the beginning of college. Road trip!

Chapter 14
All Things Must Pass

Youth moves quickly. You're there, you experience it,
and then it's gone. Did you enjoy it?

Kelly and Tuck took off from Tallytown in Tuck's silver '70s Mustang. The '70s Mustangs looked nothing like the '60s Mustangs. Ford still made them smaller than most cars, but they tried to make them look sleek and dynamic with body lines up and down the fenders. The car they were bringing back was a huge, powder blue Chevrolet that should have been in the junkyard by now. But it was still running and Tuck's cousin obviously wanted to be rid of it.

Kelly and Tuck spent the first night in New Orleans, traipsing up and down Bourbon Street. They were looking for Pat O'Brian's to get their free and etched hurricane drinking glass. Pat O'Brian's was a little bit off of Bourbon Street, but they found it and loaded up with a couple hurricanes on the outdoor patio. The plan was to make it to Fort Worth the next day, so they made it an early night.

On the way back to the hotel, one of New Orleans' native sons approached Kelly and told him, "I know where you got 'dem shoes." Kelly said, "No way you know that." The accoster said, "I bet you ten bucks I know where you got 'dem shoes. I let your friend hold my ten dollahs and you let him hold your ten dollahs." The money was handed to Tuck and Kelly said, "OK?" The street gamer replied, "You got 'dem shoes on Bourbon Street on August 28, 1979." Tuck laughingly handed over the two ten-dollar bills to the prankster. Kelly had been 'gamed'.

Kelly and Tuck got up early the next morning as the sun was

rising over the Mississippi River Bridge. There was no commuter traffic yet on I-10 as they headed west to Texas. I was about an 8 hour drive so they arrived to Fort Worth with plenty of daylight left. They would be staying for a couple days with Tuck's cousin Rebecca and her husband Tom. They lived in a ramshackle wooden house with plenty of surrounding land. The sky blue Chevrolet Bel Air was out in the yard. It looked like it should be junked, but apparently it ran great.

The plan was for Tuck to drive the Chevy back to Tallytown and Kelly would follow in Tuck's Mustang. But first they would stay a few days with Tuck's cousin, hang out, and go to a Rangers baseball game. The only method of body washing in the old house was a large bathtub with no curtain or shower door. Before going to the Ranger game, Kelly drew his bathwater and laid out in the tub. He was lathering a large bar of soap on his body and in walked Rebecca. The house was so old there was no lock on the bathroom door. Kelly thought about it at the time, but figured no one would accidently enter. "Oh, sorry, sorry, sorry," she exclaimed with open fingers across her eyes.

Kelly was mildly amused as he had noticed Rebecca looking at him during dinner and other times during the day. Apparently she wanted to look some more. All was out in the open for her private viewing as she reversed course and left the bathroom. Kelly laughed about it to himself, and the incident was never mentioned. It was best that way, as Tom may not have been so amused.

The next day Tuck and Kelly fired up the two vehicles to head down to Port Arthur. Kelly had his misgivings about the POS Bel Air making it very far, but he followed the ancient Bel Air in Tuck's Mustang. Tuck said his goodbyes to his cousin and her family. Kelly wanted to give a wink to Rebecca but he restrained himself in case Tom was looking.

The trip south was uneventful until the duo reached the steep Beaumont Bridge. Coming down the south side of the bridge almost to Port Arthur the brakes went out on the prehistoric Chevy 'boat'. This was a scary situation for Tuck because the bridge had a 40-degree decline. Tuck put the car into its lowest gear while pumping the brakes for any stopping power remaining. Kelly had no idea that anything was awry until Tuck pulled over after coming off the bridge.

Tuck yelled from a spot in the grass, "The brakes went out! I thought I was gonna die!" Kelly asked, "Can you drive slow? We're almost there." Tuck said, "I think so. So off they went at a snail's pace. Tuck was able to slow the beast at a few red lights and the two made it to Aunt June's house on the Sabine River.

The Mustang had Florida plates on it and that attracted the neighborhood teen friends of Kelly's cousins. "Who's here from Florida? We want to meet them!" the kids asked. Kelly didn't realize that people from Florida were celebrities in Texas. Once the teenagers met Kelly and Tuck in person, they all returned to earth and went their separate ways.

Kelly and Tuck were given sleeping quarters in an internal room that had no windows. They slept through the night and into the next day as no sun or alarms were there to awake them. When they finally did wake up it was around noon. Kelly asked his aunt, "Why didn't you wake us up?" "Oh, we figured we'd let you catch up on your shuteye," Kelly's aunt responded.

It was now lunchtime as the multitude of cousins and friends crowded the dining room table and the adjoining family room. Kelly's younger cousin Amanda was there along with her friend Anita. Guess what? Anita was a natural white blonde with looks that could kill. Kelly was in immediate trouble, but you only live once. No one was interested in Tuck due to his thick glasses and lispy speech. That turned the microscope to Kelly.

Tuck had to find a brake mechanic for fixing the Chevy and that task took all day. Meanwhile Kelly sat between Amanda and Anita on the river wall, sipping on Cokes that graduated into beers. Aunt June and her doctor husband were very liberal with their teenage kids. By the time they had their final two children, Amanda and Lander, there were no more rules.

Amanda had an idea that the group should take a drive north to Nacogdoches and stay in their lake cabin. This would be a detour from Tuck's original plan, but he was game. The next morning three cars drove north out of Port Arthur. Tuck was in the newly repaired Chevy Bel Air, Kelly in the Mustang, with Amanda and Anita bringing up the rear in a VW microbus. The girls hung their cigarettes out the windows and smoked the whole way up. The microbus probably experienced some different smoking paraphernalia as well.

The cabin was an obvious party place with a high ceiling in the living area, one large bedroom/bathroom upstairs, and two bedrooms downstairs. A canoe was out on the lake dock for quick trips onto the water. Kelly and Anita made a rowing excursion by themselves giggling and gazing the whole time. "Wow!" thought Kelly, "This is moving fast!" And he wasn't referring to the canoe.

When they returned from canoeing, Amanda had a big pot of spaghetti ready for dinner. Kelly wanted to get a mild beer buzz going first, so they waited a bit on dinner, sitting in the backyard screened porch. No one was starving anyway. After dinner everyone was done in. Amanda and Anita would share the upstairs bedroom and Kelly and Tuck would have their own rooms downstairs. But first there were cards. Spades was the game of the house. It was very similar to Hearts, so Kelly picked it up right away. After a few more beers, the group wandered off to bed.

As the sun was starting to beam into Kelly's bedroom window, his door opened and there was Anita in a slip and panties. Kelly had a good idea where this was going, but he first informed Anita that he had to visit "John." Luckily Anita knew what this meant and waited for him. Anita liked control and made everything right by being on top. Both parties were happy with the outcome and Anita snuck back to her bedroom.

Later that morning, Tuck and Kelly said their goodbyes and drove the county roads back to the civilization of I-10. They only made it to a "no tell motel" in Pensacola while the Chevy behaved the whole way.

Upon returning to Tally, Chuck parked the sky-blue eyesore in the fraternity parking lot and Kelly went back to his apartment in preparation for fall studies. He was also preparing to give Gloria some bad news. She would have to come and pick up her things stored in Kelly's closet. The cracked voice on the other end seemed to anticipate the worst. Gloria's absence for the whole summer created a knowledge that reverberated into Kelly's ear from the phone. But he couldn't tell her over the telephone. It had to be in person.

Chapter 15
New Beginnings Open up a New World

People are like the bougainvillea.
Beautiful flowers on the surface may hide deadly thorns underneath.

Kelly felt terrible, but it was a road he had to cross. Due to her glumness at Kelly's apartment Gloria may have seen it coming, but she didn't let on as she moved her belongings to her car. Kelly finally told her, "Gloria, I think we should go our separate ways." There was no good way to convey this. What are the alternatives? "We should date other people." Lame. "Let's be friends." Hollow. Being away from each other for so long didn't work for Kelly. He wanted to see his girlfriend every day. Of course Gloria chalked it up to Kelly finally getting what he wanted from her and then moving on. Kelly was sure the roles would be reversed in his future encounters, and he would be tossed aside by someone he really cared for. Stand by.

Kelly's fraternity brother and nearby neighbor Joe had a friend from home that was coming back to school after a hiatus. Dan had been admitted to the university, but needed a place to live. Joe knew about Herbert leaving the fold and getting his own place. This left a vacancy in Kelly and Johnboy's apartment. It was settled: Dan would take the vacant bedroom/dining room for the fall quarter.

Dan could be a bit brash and loud sometimes, especially after a few beers, but he and Kelly meshed really well. They got along in the after school hours and at the apartment. One of Dan's favorite things to do at the apartment complex was to jump off the second floor patio that adjoined the pool area. There was a wood railing that would be climbed over, planting your feet onto the cement on the other side of the rail. Then the second floor jump across the pool deck chairs and into the water ensued. One small miscalculation and the jumper's head would hit the coping on the side of the pool.

A number of the complex's residents would try this dangerous feat, and luckily all were successful. Kelly took it one step further and would dive head and arms first into the deep end. This was especially dangerous as the head would be the first thing to hit if the water was missed. The other feat was to stand on the top of the railing, pound your chest like Tarzan, wait for the pool crowd to notice you, and jump from the *top* of the wooden rail. As the warmer season was letting go and fall was arriving, the wooden railing became more rickety. This didn't stop the jumpers even though it should have. If the rail were to collapse mid-jump the jumper would crash down onto solid concrete or worse yet the fencing around the pool. Fortunately, that event did not occur prior to the cold season arriving. The next spring, management replaced the wooden railing with sturdy timbers. The office manager found out about the jumping and berated the guilty. Kelly's response was, "Yeah, OK."

Kelly had met a science class friend named Jonathan who was aiming to be a dentist. Sometimes Kelly would drive over to Jonathan's apartment across town, hang out and listen to music. Jonathan loved to blast AC/DC at an eleven on the stereo scale from his downstairs apartment. This was before AC/DC was well known and when Bon Scott was the frontman. Jonathan's complex was having a goodbye to summer event around their apartment pool. Jonathan had had a few too many. He crawled up onto the top of the pool house roof. It was a good fifteen feet from there to the pool water, but Jonathan tried it anyway. Disaster struck, Jonathan hit the side of the pool, and had to be medevacked to the hospital. Fortuitously, Jonathan recovered and attended school that fall. His reaction was always, "No big deal, what's the problem?" Kelly never jumped off his second floor pool deck again.

The tenants in the apartment underneath that of Kelly, John-boy, and now Dan were changing this fall. Three young ladies moved into Kelly's old downstairs apartment. They didn't use the dining room as a bedroom, but Rhonda and Cynthia resided together with twin beds in the master. Lacey had Kelly's old room by herself. Rhonda was a large, brown-haired girl who seemed to be in charge of the flat. It wasn't overt, but present all the same. Cynthia was a skinny blonde who was quiet, demure and subservient to the other girls. Lacey was a short voluptuous 5'2" with dark brown hair and an outgoing attitude. Kelly would sometimes see a combination of two or more of the downstairs girls walking back from class. He was especially observant of Lacey's tight lime-green shorts that were pulled up to the point that body curves both front and back were visible.

Lacey made it perfectly clear over and over that she had a boyfriend from back home in Jacksonville. However, he had decided to attend the University of South Carolina instead of staying with Lacey during college. Hmmm, was this a crack in Lacey's armor? All the guys made fun of the mascot for South Carolina known as the Gamecock. One can imagine the verbal gyrations of that word.

As it were, Lacey maintained her stance and her distance from any advances. So, one evening in Kelly's apartment everyone had seemed to go out on a Friday night except for him and the downstairs occupant Cynthia. The two sat in Kelly's living room watching a small, black and white TV with the required rabbit ears on top. The couch was green vinyl that was always either too hot or too cold. It seemed that plastic vinyl seating was the rage in those days.

Cynthia was not overly pretty, but she had a thin body, decent face, and of course the requisite blonde hair. Kelly figured that Cynthia would be receptive towards him due to her ordinary looks. He leaned in for a kiss, but she played hard to get, and backed out. A few minutes later Kelly began to rub her shoulders. This went well and then he was able to land a lip kiss with Cynthia. She seemed undecided about the kiss, and later Kelly found out this was due to her inexperience with any guys. Apparently no one had noticed her nor pursued her in high school.

Kelly didn't know this and decided to go for broke. He asked Cynthia to retire to his bedroom. Her reaction was to immediately head for the front door and to leave Kelly on his own. Kelly was dumbfounded by this rejection and didn't know how to react or even if he should react.

Anger overwhelmed Kelly and he stomped off to his bedroom. The rage continued to escalate while lying on the king size mattress. Kelly began screaming into his pillow and then out the opened window. Cynthia and Rhonda also had their bedroom window open directly below Kelly's room. Rhonda calmly called out the window up to Kelly, "Kelly, are you alright? What's the matter?" Kelly responded in his fury, "I hate her! I hate her!" Was Kelly referring to his biological mother Liza or to Cynthia? Psychologically it was a toss-up. Rhonda offered to come up and calm him down, which she did. Kelly did relax in Rhonda's presence but he was still hurting. Kelly was not attracted to Rhonda but he always remembered her gesture of comforting him when she didn't have to.

Kelly had to hit the books hard this fall as he was entering into the meat of his major: Biology and Chemistry. These majors required a multitude of laboratory classes that took many Friday afternoons while others were out having fun. Kelly had signed up for fifteen weekly hours of classes that fall, but with two laboratory classes, it added up to twenty-one on-site hours. This would take a lot of studying and less socializing on his part.

Physics was also a tough course that Kelly attended with Jonathan. Jonathan was pre-dental and didn't need the grades that Kelly required. So Jonathan would drift off in class inking song lyrics onto the desktop table. His favorite artistic lettering was a combination of "Wang Dang Sweet Poontang" and "Yank Me Crank Me, But Dontcha Wake Me Up and Dontcha Thank Me." Luckily the prof didn't notice Johnboy making his Ted Nugent Sharpie markings.

While waiting outside the locked door for the Physics professor, Kelly noticed a dirty blonde-haired girl. In one-of-a-kind fashion she was holding a German Shephard's leash. This was in a time before service dogs. Kelly jokingly asked her, "Is that your classmate?" She replied, "Yep, he is my protection from random miscreant people." Kelly took this as a challenge. He then saw her male companion looking unpleasantly at him. Kelly asked the nice looking tall blonde, "Is that your boyfriend?" She replied "No" while the male friend looked even more disdainful and bothered by Kelly. It was obvious that the male accompanier wanted her to reply "Yes, he is my boyfriend." But that didn't happen. The classroom door was unlocked and opened up at that point. Kelly didn't pursue her smiling friendliness, but the thought was there for the rest of the quarter. Jealous boy didn't take his eyes off of Kelly in case Kelly tried anything. Not to worry.

Johnboy returned from his summer stay with his parents. They had moved to the well-heeled Palm Beach, but they still had Johnboy work during his time off from school. Johnboy worked as a hotel desk concierge where he met a lot of people. One of those people was a female he surprisingly showed up with for the fall quarter. Johnboy's plan was for her to live in his bedroom, but no extra rent was provided for her presence. When Kelly and Dan brought this up, Johnboy defended her by saying she cleaned the kitchen and vacuumed the rug. There was not much else to do all day with no job and no schooling. The girl was obviously a night worker, something that Johnboy eventually admitted. Now the pressure was really on. "Get her out of here!" Dan and Kelly persistently stated. One weekend well into the fall quarter Johnboy finally drove her back to Palm Beach and returned without her.

During the quarter, Dan began to take a dislike toward Johnboy. When Johnboy was around, which wasn't very often, Dan would start with snide remarks that made fun of Johnboy's offbeat personality and actions. One Saturday night Kelly and Dan were returning to the apartment from Fred's Backdoor Lounge. Fred's was becoming a routine as the bartenders would immediately mix up a rum and coke upon seeing Kelly enter the bar. The trend toward video game machines was evident at Fred's. There were no pinball machines to be found. It was the trendy place to go.

On the sidewalk outside of Johnboy's second floor window, Dan noticed the light on in Johnboy's room. "Let's get him to come to the window and then hide," said Dan. At that Dan took out a penny and threw it at Johnboy's window. The penny did not have its intended effect of tapping the window. The penny went right through the glass without cracking it. The outcome of the toss was a penny-sized hole in the glass. Kelly and Dan hid in the bushes, laughing while Johnboy looked outside and inspected the strange damage.

The next day Johnboy notified the site manager about the incident. The manager came over and took a look at the hole. When he got back to his office, the manager proceeded to call the police. The theory was that the hole was made by a bullet. When Kelly took a closer look at the hole, he could see the grounds for that conclusion. The next day a city police officer came knocking at the door. The first thing on Kelly's mind was the pot plants growing in the hanging planter by the window.

The policeman took no notice of the plants and proceeded to Johnboy's bedroom. The officer looked at the hole in the window and then went to the other side of the room with a flashlight. He pointed the flashlight at the wall and closet where the trajectory of a bullet would have taken it. No bullet was found. The officer wrote a quick report, left it with Kelly, and went back to his beat. Kelly read the note which stated that the incident was closed with no firm conclusion. Johnboy later dropped the note off with the complex manager. Within a week the Dramedy Club apartment company replaced Johnboy's window and it was never discussed again.

One day later in the fall quarter, Dan and Joe needed some transportation and Johnboy kindly lent them his Camaro. The friends conveyed their needed items and returned the car to Johnboy. Little did he know that the boys had played a trick on him. After about three days of his car sitting in the warm sun, Johnboy began to complain about the fact that his car was emitting a rotted smell. Dan snickered a bit at that but let it go. When Johnboy left, Dan owned up to Kelly that he and Joe had left a raw chicken under the spare tire in the trunk.

Johnboy continued to complain to his roommates about the stench in his car. Kelly understood the joke, because Johnboy was such an exacting perfectionist about almost everything, especially when it came to what he called his "chick magnet," the red Camaro. Kelly and Dan continued to ignore the grumbles until one day Johnboy came home livid. He said, "I went to my gas station and the attendant helped me find the stink in my car! It was rotting chicken!" Kelly and Dan continued to deny any knowledge of what had happened. Kelly thought to himself, "If I was Johnboy, it would be obvious to me that Dan and Joe had borrowed my car and they were the culprits."

Somehow a girl named Judy got the blame from Johnboy. Judy hung out by the pool sometimes and observed Johnboy preening, looking at his compact mirror, and reading *Playboy* magazine. She took offense to all of these actions and more. There was a genuine dislike, if not hate, between the two. Judy was, for the time being, girlfriend to Hernando. Kelly could not understand that hook up but the future would tell their outcome. Kelly didn't want to defend Judy or get involved at all, but wasn't it obvious that Judy never had Johnboy's car keys? And who had? Duhhh!

Kelly would still attend home football games with the PiPhi's at Doak Campbell Stadium. Their section was packed assholes to elbows, but here came Nora with her chunky blonde roommate. Nora had long dirty golden locks down to her behind. She made a beeline to Kelly, pushing her way through the fraternity brothers. Butts were slid to make room for the girls on the bleacher. Nora plopped down next to Kelly and drunkenly said, "Hello!" Kelly was amused and flattered at the same time. He had met Nora before at the house as she was a recent little sister.

After the football game, which was another win for Bobby Bowden, the two female roommates and Kelly walked to their nearby apartment. Nora was very touchy feely on the way. When they got to the upstairs apartment, Nora's roommate disappeared. Nora pulled out her Led Zeppelin albums which were played while the two lounged on the living room sofa drinking a beer. Kelly wasn't sure where the penchant for that band came from, but Nora was a big fan. Every time Kelly visited later that fall, either *Led Zeppelin I, II,* or *IV* was played.

The two fell asleep in Nora's room that Saturday night, but sleep came immediately and lasted until the sun rose. The next morning both were a bit disheveled, but Nora and her long, thick hair had taken the brunt. Kelly walked the half mile home in the cool morning air.

Kelly wasn't much for phone calling girls, but he made an exception with Nora. "Are you going to the football game this weekend? Let's meet up before the game," he propositioned. And so it was. Kelly drove over to Nora's place and game preparations (imbibing) began. Nora was pretty tight by the time they headed off, walking to the game. The two squeezed into the PiPhi seating and cheered when Osceola and Renegade stuck the spear onto midfield. The chanting of school and fraternity mantras were repeated throughout the game. The results of the evening were pretty much the same as last time: a Seminole win, a walk back to Nora's place, listening to Led Zeppelin and sleeping through the night. There was no intimacy as Nora always passed out first and Kelly would help her to bed and knock out himself.

On the third "date" Kelly invited Nora out for dinner, which she naturally accepted. They ended up back at Kelly's place. Again Nora passed out, but this time in Kelly's monster-sized bed. Kings were unheard of during those college days. Some students had Queen beds, but never a King.

The next morning Nora woke up with her tousled look and a mild hangover. Kelly wanted to make love by this point, but Nora was hesitant. Kelly nagged and pleaded that morning and finally Nora succumbed. She probably had experience with what would happen next. Kelly was not ready for a girlfriend and the silence between them became deafening. Kelly didn't call and Nora didn't call. A few months later at the university library Kelly was looking for a certain book and emerged from the eight-foot shelves. There was Nora sitting at a wooden table studying. She had drastically shortened her unruly locks to the top of her shoulders. Nora didn't see Kelly (or acted so). Kelly did a 180 back to the book racks never to see Nora again.

Chapter 16
Is It Time to Settle Down?

Knuckling down doesn't mean knuckling under.

It was amazing that Kelly had kept his grades remarkable and had so much fun along the way. He attributed it to six days of hard, sober learning and one day of fun and frolicking. Kelly had grown his hair out over the last few months. It was over his ears and over his collar. This was no longer the style, so he hiked up the hill outside his apartment to the genderless hair cutting salon. When he emerged from the modern and expensive salon (twelve dollars for a haircut?!), Kelly had a flattop on his crown, ears absent of any hair covering, and a long tapered mane over his collar. Was this the contemporary new style known as the mullet? Business in front, party in back!

School became the priority for his junior year. Class subjects were getting tougher and tougher as he moved into his major. Girls were now a second thought; however he still had an eye on Lacey. She continued to flaunt her towel-fluffy short shorts around the complex. When Kelly spoke with Lacey she always brought up her boyfriend back home. She said, "I can't wait to see him when I go home for Christmas." It wasn't clear if Lacey was trying to convince Kelly, or convince herself. Kelly was in no rush, but he knew that "absence makes the heart grow fonder" (of someone else).

Kelly did well in all his classes for the next two quarters, except for Organic Chemistry I and Organic Chemistry II. He pulled a "hook" (C) in both. Kelly knew these grades would be scrutinized during his interviews for medical school. Achieving a passing grade did not allow him to retake the classes and re-place the grades. Kelly's dad, Kelly Sr. had received an F when he first took Organic, and was able to retake the class and replace the F with his newly-earned grade of A. This certainly helped Kelly Sr. get into optometry school.

Two years of differential and integral calculus, anatomical biology, physics, along with organic and chemistry/microbiology lab classes were very time consuming, and brain consuming as well. The fraternity kept a file cabinet full of old tests from various classes. Some lazy profs reused the same tests they had given in previous years. Most of the old tests in the file were useless due to age and subject. Theatre 101 tests were useless to Kelly. Certainly there were no organic or physics tests in the files. Kelly was on his own, as it should be.

After the holiday break, everyone returned to a cold Tally-town. There were no more short shorts on the girls and no more hiked up tennis shorts on the guys. It was cold by Floridian standards and everyone bundled up.

Kelly saw Lacey walking to class one day, looking serious and somewhat forlorn. They traded pleasantries for a bit and then the seriousness slipped out; Lacey's boyfriend was seeing someone else at his college. She tried to defend that it wasn't serious, but Kelly could tell that it hadn't gone well over the break. Kelly saw a crack in the ice, but decided to stay aloof and focus on his studies.

The winter drudgery moved along. Lacey became friendlier when Kelly saw her walking to class one day. He decided to use the old familiar line, "How about lunch at the Union Square cafeteria?" She replied with a meek, "OK, what time?" The lunch went well and they were now graduating from the acquaintance phase to the friendship phase. Kelly wouldn't mind if it went further, but time would tell.

Since their apartments were so close, Kelly and Lacey would visit each other for a talk or a meal. They were progressing from the friendship phase to the courting phase. They began studying together at Kelly's living room table. One day, studying was on neither of their minds. Kelly began playing footsy with Lacey underneath the table. He thought, "I wonder how far up her leg I can go?" I turned out that his socked foot made it all the way up. There was an instant understanding between the two as they moved to Kelly's room. It had progressed from the courting phase to the intimacy phase.

Lacey had no inhibitions unlike Kelly what had experienced before. Everything was on the table. The two became exclusive, and though it wasn't formally stated, they dated no others. It seemed as both were exploring anything they could possibly think of. Life became calm and well-balanced over the next few months.

That spring Kelly was hard at work with his studies, but he had a significant event looming. The MCAT medical school exam was to be given at the end of May. Kelly tried to add those study preparations to his daily curriculum, but wasn't too successful as the test had changed from previous versions. His friends goaded him to hire a tutor, but Kelly couldn't afford that. There was no online coursework during those times. The cost of the test alone was formidable enough for a "scraping-by" college student.

The Friday night before the MedCat test (as it was called back then), Kelly decided to turn in early and get a good night's sleep. Sometimes the best laid plans go awry and this was one of those. Cynthia and Rhonda from downstairs had pledged as little sisters to a fraternity. The two new initiates decided to invite the frat over to their apartment and celebrate.

Kelly had just fallen asleep upstairs as the party noise erupted. Loud music, yelling, and a drunken celebration was vibrating Kelly's bedroom. This had never happened in all the months that the girls lived downstairs. Kelly was at first unbelieving, but then anger overwhelmed him. He had a big day tomorrow and this racket could go on all night.

Kelly sat up in bed, deciding what to do. He marched down the stairs and into the open-doored apartment. Throngs of guys and girls littered the downstairs apartment. They were in the living room, the kitchen, and both bedrooms. The largest congregation appeared to be in Rhonda and Cynthia's bedroom, directly below Kelly's bedroom.

Kelly began yelling at the mass of partiers, "Hey! Keep it down! I have the MedCat test tomorrow!" The males looked at Kelly and then at the girls as if to say, "Who is this lunatic? Should we take him seriously?" Kelly went into Lacey's room where there were frat boys, unknown girls, and Lacey. "This is my girlfriend! What are you doing in here?" A bit of jealous emotion showed in Kelly's outburst.

Kelly marched back upstairs. The party kept going for a while but soon fizzled out and quieted down. The heated rage didn't allow Kelly to fall back asleep for a few hours. Thinking back, the party might have ended well before he finally calmed down enough to invite sleep.

Kelly got up bleary-eyed and staggered over to the science auditorium for his MCAT testing. The test would take all day, so he hoped his mind would come around after its lack of sleep. Kelly was hopeful, but wasn't that confident about his performance. Sure enough, his score came back mediocre: 10 out of 15. Would he take it again or try to talk his way through the medical school interviews? The test cost hundreds of dollars he didn't have. Kelly decided to live with the test results he had tallied. Was this a good decision or a mistake?

Chapter 17
Good Vibrations of Summer

I'm honestly striving compared to lying.
I'm definitely living compared to dying.

Kelly decided to stay in Tallytown that summer. He had met a botany professor who was looking for workers over the summer. She had a field of cotton on the outskirts of town that was growing for her experiments and institutional studies.

The literal cotton-picking job wouldn't start for another two weeks, so Kelly had some time on his hands. It turned out that his cousins in Texas were planning a road trip to Colorado during Kelly's free time. If he could get to Port Arthur they would drive to, from, and all around Colorado. Kelly would be back in time to pick cotton. This was going to work out perfectly, or was it?

Kelly decided he would drive the Pimpo solo from Tallytown to Texas. Kelly got up early one morning with his jeans, jacket, and tennis shoes packed in the trunk. He made the non-stop (except for gas and bathroom breaks) trek across north Florida, south Alabama, south Mississippi, Louisiana, and into Texas all in one day.

Kelly's cousins and friends were all ex-hippies that would caravan west the next day. Kelly got a good night's sleep in the enclosed, no window guest room and was up raring to go the next morning. It seemed that the herb-loving crew were a bit foggy-headed until later in the day. This gave Kelly a chance to augment his camping gear. His cousin Amanda was not able to go on the trip, but she had a brand new two-person tent and a sleeping bag that she generously lent to Kelly. Amanda implored Kelly to make sure he brought the equipment back clean and in one piece. Amanda couldn't help with Kelly's lack of hiking boots, but he would make do.

Later that day he and his cousins and their friends headed out in a station wagon Subaru across Texas, into New Mexico, and then took a right turn into western Colorado. The trip took all night as they had not left East Texas until late in the afternoon.

He saw nothing but snowcapped mountains all around when Kelly woke up the next morning in the backseat of a moving vehicle. "Where am I?" he thought and then it came flooding back. Kelly blurted out to those in the front seat upon his morning wakefulness, "Just remember 'Wherever you go, there you are.'"

There was a specific camping spot outside of Ouray that the group was familiar with. The caravan headed there and set up camp. Kelly brought out the pristine tent and set it up by the bubbling creek. He unwrapped the unused sleeping bag and laid it out inside the tent for the upcoming night. Kelly's older cousin Layla had a male friend on the trip who had no tent to sleep in. Mark asked Kelly if he could use the other side of his two-person tent and Kelly agreed.

A fair amount of drinking occurred that evening around the campfire. Bottles of JD were passed around and Mark got hammered. Later in the evening everyone crawled into their tents to sleep off the liquor and prepare for the next day's hike.

Mark was passed out in Amanda's tent when Kelly got there. Wait, what was that smell? Mark was sleeping in a pile of puke. Kelly yelled, "Get out of here!" Mark somberly (not soberly) left the tent and spent the night uncovered next to the fire. Kelly did his best to clean up any droppings on the tent floor, but the darkness prevented a thorough cleaning. He rolled over to keep his face away from the stench and got some shuteye.

The plan for the next day was to start a hike to Telluride from their camp near Ouray. The tents and sleeping bags were strapped to backpacks and the uphill trudge began. The first few miles was a well-defined dirt road, and then it turned into a trail. The group found themselves at the bottom of a U-shaped crater where it wasn't obvious which way to go. There were various trails going up different parts of the mountainous surroundings. The group decided on an eastbound trail which made little sense to Kelly since Telluride was west of Ouray. When they got to the crest, the group looked out on a barren emptiness that was not Telluride. Kelly disgustedly thought, "Told ya so."

The group had to backtrack down the mountain and chose a westward trail to pursue. Hallelujah! It turned out this was the correct way. Once the mountain pass was attained, they looked down onto a green forest with a small town miles in the distance. This had to be Telluride.

The whole time they were hiking, Kelly was taking grief about wearing his tennis shoes on such a serious hike. Everyone else was wearing rough and tough hiking boots with woolen socks underneath. Once the treeline was attained, most of the group was exhausted and wanted to set up camp. Two of the male hiker friends decided to continue on to Telluride and sleep in a comfy hotel.

The rest of the group threw off their framed backpacks and sat down on large boulders. They took off their boots complaining of sore feet with blisters. Kelly had no such maladies on his feet and made sure that everyone making fun of his sneakers was visibly aware of his happy feet.

The next day Telluride was achieved and the afternoon was spent in the hotel bar looking out onto the touristy street. There were no cell phones at the time, so everyone had agreed to meet up at the Floradora Saloon. A van had been driven from Ouray to Telluride in a roundabout fashion to get everyone back to the cars they had left across the mountain.

After visiting a number of other Colorado locations, the crew headed back on the long drive to Texas. Kelly was grateful not to have to sleep anymore in a puke-smelly tent. Upon returning the camping equipment to Amanda, Kelly had to eat crow and tell her the bad news. Kelly never heard if Amanda had reused the tent or not.

Kelly headed back to the university to work for his botany professor in the cotton fields. It turned out she wanted the buds of the cotton plants picked for her microscopic studies. In the summer the buds had popped out on the six-foot plants, but the actual white cotton bolls wouldn't bloom until the fall. Kelly tried to get to the field early so that the heat and the humidity were still bearable. However, when picking the buds at that early hour, the plants were dripping wet. Kelly would come out of the fields soaked to the bone.

The student employees would bring out their crop to the picnic tables under the coolness of the trees. On the tables they would razor cut the buds open and place them on microscope glass for the professor's perusal. Kelly would perform these tasks each morning and then return to his apartment for an afternoon of poolside tanning. After 3:00 when the girls were done tanning, the guys looked around and saw no females. At that point the guys left too. In the evenings Kelly would accompany some guys from across the complex's parking lot to the Backdoor Lounge for drinks. These guys would later become Kelly's roommates during the following summer. But we get ahead of ourselves.

Lacey had again returned to Jacksonville that June to work her summer job while staying rent-free at her parents' house. Kelly was a little nervous that she would see her old boyfriend, but it sounded like old memories at this point. Anyhow, Kelly had his eye on someone new in Lacey's absence.

Word at the poolside was that Judy had broken up with Hernando. Kelly never really understood what Judy had seen in Hernando's acne scarred face and his limited English, but sometimes these matters have no explanation. Judy began enjoying her newfound freedom by hanging out at the pool in the daytime and Fred's Lounge in the nighttime. Judy had a frail, thin body, but a very cute face. Kelly would pick a lounge chair next to Judy's when he finished cotton picking for the morning. Judy's pink body had not become tan yet, but she had all summer.

Judy would visit Kelly's place and admire his wooden box now full of records. Kelly would visit Judy's place to disinterestedly watch *General Hospital*. The girls loved it when Rick Springfield would make his doctoral rounds at the hospital.

Judy had a penchant for the "green" and afterwards would come over to Kelly's for relaxation and company. The good company led to more and soon the two were a pair. How was this going to work when Lacey returned after the summer? Amazingly, providence provided Kelly a phone call one day. Lacey would not return to attend school in the fall. Kelly wondered after the call, "Did I just break up with her or did she break up with me?"

No matter, Judy and Kelly were now attached at the hip. However, smooth sailing always had its impending waves. Hernando invaded Judy's apartment one evening, angry and likely drunk. Kelly didn't think Hernando would touch Judy, so he left and went back to his place. The likely outcome if Kelly had stayed was a fistfight initiated by either Kelly or Hernando. Kelly wanted no part of that.

Later that evening a knock came at Kelly's door. It was a teary-eyed Judy escorted by her roommate. Judy came in and her roommate, seeing that Judy was safe, went back to their apartment. Judy stayed with Kelly for a night of tenderness that he would never forget. The relationship was now forged. Would it be forged in steel or aluminum?

Fall had arrived and Kelly was all signed up and ready to finish his senior year. But Judy didn't sign up for school and wasn't going to attend. Had she permanently withdrawn from college? How was she supporting herself, paying for her apartment, and paying for her red Monte Carlo? Judy was noncommittal on these points, but Kelly assumed her parents still thought she was in school and she needed their support.

Kelly spent most of his nights in the library studying. Judy was loyal to Kelly and they spent all of their extra time with each other. Judy didn't hold back from Kelly, except for one thing she was saving for marriage: the female orgasm. Kelly didn't understand depriving oneself of that ultimate pleasure, but she was adamant. Kelly didn't mind at first, as long as he was satisfied in their loving. Eventually it started to bother Kelly, but it never happened and eventually he stopped complaining.

The two maintained their relationship for the remaining school year. Kelly would have to get up early for 8am classes. On his way he would pass Judy's apartment and notice her car was not parked outside in its usual place. There was no way Judy was up this early as she always slept in with no classes or job. Kelly's fear began to permeate his brain. When he asked Judy if she had stayed out all night, her response was always, "Oh I didn't want drive from my friend's house in a bad state." Kelly noticed that Judy's roommate's car was also gone in the mornings, so he rationalized that the two were just having fun together.

One night at Kelly's apartment table, Judy brought out a little plastic bag and her compact mirror. She poured out the white contents of the small bag onto the mirror. A razor appeared and lines of the white powder were drawn on the mirror. Judy asked Kelly, "Do you have a Bic pen?" Kelly found one in the kitchen drawer and brought it out to her. She pulled the ink chamber out of the plastic cover with her teeth. She removed the blue plastic stopper out from the other end. The plastic cover of the pen transformed into a sturdy, rigid straw. Judy applied the "straw" to her nostril and began sniffing the white lines. She left one line remaining and gestured the straw toward Kelly. Kelly seriously refused and crossed his arms. Kelly was very anti-drugs as he considered even weed, much less white powder, in conflict with his goals.

It became clear to Kelly that the narcotic was allowing Judy to pay her bills and explained where she was late at night. When a sale was processed, a mutual use between the seller and the buyer ensued. The drug prevented any sleep. The only question in Kelly's mind was, "What else happened between the buyer and the seller?" His thoughts ran wild. "Maybe more money was involved for other activities."

Kelly and Judy stayed together for his senior year as the white powder event happened late in the school year. Even after that Judy attended Kelly's graduation along with Kelly's parents. Kelly decided to stay and work in Tally for the summer. With this knowledge, Judy decided to end it with Kelly. Even though Kelly was suspicious of her activities, he was devastated. Usually it was Kelly doing the dirty work of disconnection, not the other way around.

Chapter 18

The Summer of His Discontent

Stuff happens causing a correction to the steering wheel.
Sometimes it's a slow turning, other times it's a quick jerk.

Kelly had an interview for medical school with Mrs. Hoffner. There was no med school at his university, however, so some students were sent to the University in Gainesville for their four years of doctoral training. Mrs. Hoffner focused on the issues that Kelly was expecting. His overall GPA of 3.4, his MCAT test result, and the two Cs in organic chemistry. Kelly was able to satisfactorily explain those issues; however, he wasn't expecting her question out of left field: "What do you consider to be your best quality and your poorest quality for completing medical school?" Kelly was honest, but a little too honest in his answer. He replied that he was very studious and that his father and grandfather were good models in that they had achieved their medical degrees. He replied to the second part of the question with the statement, "I like to socialize with others." Unfortunately, in his honesty, he used the word "party" instead of "socialize." The interview was pretty much over at that point. Kelly received a DECLINE letter in the mail the following week.

Kelly had also applied to two other medical schools, Emory and Howard. Howard immediately rejected him, but the very expensive Emory took a few weeks to decline him. Kelly was accepted to the optometry school attended by his father in Memphis; however, they were full and Kelly would have to start the following year. What to do for a whole year waiting?

Since Kelly had decided to stay in town for the summer,

mostly because of Judy, his apartment room had been rented out to Joe, Kelly's frat brother and Dan's friend. It seemed that Dan had flunked out of school, but was hanging out for the summer. Sometimes word doesn't make it back to the supporting parents for a while, and the money keeps on coming.

Kelly had to move across the parking lot and live for the summer with his Backdoor Lounge friends. Invariably after work, Kelly would hear the question, "Fred's?" With no school obligations, the answer was always "Yes."

These fellows had put an actual door and frame onto their dining room, making it a real third room. This was Kelly's accommodation for the summer. Kelly's best friend Rob had the summer off from the Naval Academy and made a visit up to Tally. Kelly's roommates decided to have a party that Saturday night. They hung a bedsheet from their second floor window with the painted enticement, "Party Here Tonight."

It seemed as if half the complex showed up that night. Of course it was summer so a lot of the student population was out of town, but there was an overflow down the stairs and into some of the surrounding apartments. The plan was for Rob to crash in a sleeping bag on Kelly's floor. Kelly spent the latter half of the night sitting on the couch and talking with a girl named Deanna. He had seen Dee, as she was called, around the pool area, but never got to speak with her. Dee was blonde, of course, and had a curvaceous body.

It was getting late and somehow Kelly and Dee ended up in his bedroom/dining room quarters with the door closed. Dee kicked off her shoes and one thing led to another. Rob had been talking with everyone until the party died down. He opened Kelly's door and in the dark he stumbled on some shoes. He muttered, "Shoes," and then more loudly, "Female shoes! About face, reverse course!" Rob had to sleep on the drink-stained couch for the night.

The next hungover morning, Rob and Kelly walked the block

up the hill to the Golden Arches. Yes, this McDonald's still had the giant yellow semicircles running from the outdoor eating area and into the sides of the restaurant. Greasy sausage and eggs on a white muffin were gorged upon to settle the stomachs. It didn't help the headaches, but hopefully the aspirin would kick in soon.

Back at the apartment, the boys were rousing slowly. The plan was to head south to Panama City. There are two things to do in PC: cruise the strip or hang out at the beach. Since it was a dudefest, the four cruised up and down the main drag looking for people (girls) to talk to. The Mercedes convertible that they were driving was an aid in getting a conversation going. But during the day, the ladies were sober. They saw the ordinary faces of Kelly's roommates and kept going.

The four hung out at the main PC beach for a couple hours, eyeing the passing bikinis. The light-skinned guys like Rob were starting to turn red. There was a beach bar within sight as they lounged on the beach. The Full Glass saloon had bar stools around tall tables. The bar was enticingly sending out signals to the boys, "Come visit me, come visit me." The four at almost the same time said, "Let's get a beer." The sun didn't set in the summer until 9:00 pm, so it would be a while before partygoers began packing the bar. The four guys hung out until then, but since they were very underdressed, they packed it in and returned to Tallytown.

Rob left the next day in his yellow Pinto after getting a good night's sleep in the previously unused sleeping bag. The green shag carpet provided additional padding for Rob's slumber.

Kelly decided to pursue Dee for a date. She was bigger than his normal partners, but he liked their first encounter. After dinner at a local restaurant, the two returned to Dee's apartment. Neither knew what was going to happen as they relaxed on Dee's couch. All of a sudden the front door opened and in walked a Middle Eastern fellow. Kelly had seen him hanging at the pool with Dee on previous occasions and assumed it was her former boyfriend. Was this becoming a routine occurrence?

The ex-boyfriend immediately lit into Dee with a jealous tirade. Dee was quiet and didn't argue back. Kelly decided to hang for a bit and see if the boyfriend would leave. He didn't. He calmed down and sat on the other side of Dee. Kelly said, "I'm outta here." Kelly saw the two together later in the summer and made the correct assumption that Dee had taken him back. Oh well, there were a lot of Goldies in the college sea.

Kelly had to get up and leave early for his cotton picking job again this summer. Even though Judy had kicked him to the curb, Kelly still looked to see if her Monte Carlo was parked where it should be. This was almost a curse, because every morning he had to pass by her apartment. More often than not, her car was not there. In the future after joining the working masses, Kelly would come back and visit friends still attending college. On those occasions Kelly would see Judy at Fred's Lounge. She was always friendly and seemed to want to end the night with Kelly. Sometimes it was easier with a known quantity. This hookup never happened but much later Judy would visit Kelly in his new work town. This was not the end.

Kelly wasn't sure what the working world was going to offer him, but its looming presence was imminent. He knew he wasn't going to stay in Tallytown, but what was out there? In a year he could attend optometry school, but what was going to happen in the meantime?

Kelly perused the want ads in the *Press Democrat* newspaper. The state government was hiring weights and measures inspectors. Kelly went through the interview process and received an offer for the opening. The position was located in South Florida for a minor salary. However, this would work because he could stay with Grandma, at least for enough time to get his feet on the ground. Kelly's dad, Kelly Sr., derided Kelly Jr. for considering such a job. Apparently Kelly Sr. had a friend who had worked the same job and hated it. There was no degree required and the pay was very low. Kelly Jr. tried to assure his dad that the position was only temporary to make ends meet and that he would attend optometry school the next fall. This reasoning didn't seem to work for Kelly Sr. Kelly Jr. knew that his dad would have to admit this outcome to his morning coffee friends. He wouldn't be able to brag about his son attending med school, or even optometry school. Kelly Sr. would have to say that his son was a disappointment. Was this going to be the case?

NOT THE END

Addendum
Kelly's Future Exploits

Don't Stay in Your Own Backyard

We all have oceans to cross
While trying to minimize our loss
There must be the heart to do it
We must avoid the desire to say 'screw it'
What do dreams know of boundaries?
We are sometimes left with indecision and quandaries
I sometimes think of the various lands stuck
to the bottom of my shoes
To visit your seven continents required paying some dues
I am grateful for a world so great
Travelling your shores and lands was my fate
Though with some reluctance on her part, the travels
included my mate
While achieving this major item on the bucket list
The memory will survive the trip into our final mist

ABOOKS

ALIVE Book Publishing and ALIVE Publishing Group
are imprints of Advanced Publishing LLC,
3200 A Danville Blvd., Suite 204, Alamo, California 94507

Telephone: 925.837.7303
alivebookpublishing.com

CPSIA information can be obtained
at www.ICGtesting.com
Printed in the USA
LVHW101605280722
724568LV00019B/121